LIBRARY WEB SITES

Creating Online Collections and Services

A. Paula Wilson

American Library Association
Chicago   2004

A. Paula Wilson is Adult Services Coordinator at the Maricopa County (Ariz.) Library District. She previously worked as the manager for virtual library services at the Las Vegas–Clark County (Nev.) Library District and as reference librarian for the Providence (R.I.) Public Library, in addition to a variety of library positions ranging from page, clerk, and marketing assistant to librarian, reference department head, and manager of web services and collections. She received an MLIS from the University of Rhode Island and a BA in political science with an emphasis in Latin American studies from Arizona State University. Wilson has been involved with professional library associations on both the state and national levels and has published articles in local newspapers and library bulletins as well as in *American Libraries* and *National Employment Weekly*. Recognized as a leader in her field, Wilson has been quoted in the *Wall Street Journal* and in *Jobs Rated Almanac*. She is the contributing editor of the "Tech Talk" column in *Public Libraries* magazine.

While extensive effort has gone into ensuring the reliability of information appearing in this book, the publisher makes no warranty, express or implied, on the accuracy or reliability of the information, and does not assume and hereby disclaims any liability to any person for any loss or damage caused by errors or omissions in this publication.

The paper used in this publication meets the minimum requirements of American National Standard for Information Sciences—Permanence of Paper for Printed Library Materials, ANSI Z39.48-1992. ∞

Library of Congress Cataloging-in-Publication Data

Wilson, A. Paula.
    Library Web sites : creating online collections and services / A. Paula Wilson.
       p. cm.
    Includes bibliographical references and index.
    ISBN 0-8389-0872-1
    1. Library Web sites. 2. Libraries—Special collections—Electronic information resources. 3. Electronic reference services (Libraries) 4. Digital libraries. I. Title.
    Z674.75.W67W55 2004
    025.04—dc22   2003021879

Printed in the United States of America

08   07   06   05   04   5   4   3   2   1

For my boys
David, Richard, and Brian

Contents

Figures

Acknowledgments

A debt of gratitude to Renée Vaillancourt McGrath, consulting editor, who had enough faith in my ability to ask me to write this book. Renée has provided much-needed guidance and encouragement along the way. I would also like to thank Eloise L. Kinney, copy editor, whose attention to detail and accuracy has helped make this book more understandable for readers. Yvette Dowling also took the time to provide me with feedback on several chapters. I thank her for her valuable comments and insight.

I would also like to extend my appreciation to staff at the Las Vegas–Clark County Library District. Their forward thinking has challenged me to discover new ways to serve customers through the Web. Additionally, I would like to express my gratitude to the library profession, especially those authors listed in the "Bibliography," who have conducted research to further the development of online services, as well as those libraries that have created exemplary sites, many of which appear in screen shots throughout this book. Books like this are not written without the help of the many people who implement new services and allow us to learn from them through discussion or literature. Thanks to those people for sharing that knowledge.

Finally, I would like to thank my husband, Brian Wilson, who kept me on track with just one word: *focus*. Without his support, this book would not exist.

Preface

This book was written for library staff as they embark on creating and upgrading web sites. It provides information on the delivery of online services and collections using the guiding principles of librarianship and established web standards to help mold library services for the future. The implementation of interactive features included in a second- and third-generation web site are explained in detail, as are current trends and issues regarding the delivery and placement of such services. This book was written for librarians who, in addition to public service, are also assigned web site responsibilities. This book also addresses public service aspects of implementing web services, which may provide technicians with a broader understanding of library services and how technology impacts them.

My position as a virtual library manager at the Las Vegas–Clark County Library District afforded me the time to address in detail many of the issues included in this book. Creating online services and collections for delivery through an award-winning web site has been the main focus of my work.* This has enabled me to work closely with a variety of staff members throughout our organization. We have learned that web work affects virtually every department in the library. This book not only represents my experiences, success, and failures, but it also gathers a great deal of pertinent library literature and represents the collective knowledge available at this time.

---

* In 2002, the Las Vegas–Clark County Library District web site, http://www.lvccld.org, received two awards: Best Large Public Library Web Site, from *netConnect (Library Journal)* and Dow Jones, and the *From Bricks to Clicks* Award, from the Technology Business Alliance of Nevada.

As we look toward the future, we cannot forget lessons learned from the past. In 1992, I began my first full-time librarian position with the Providence (R.I.) Public Library. Like most eager new library school graduates, I had many questions and wanted to learn everything! I was awed by the librarians, not just by how they could answer any questions put in front of them, but more so by the methodical way in which they answered and their ability to transfer that knowledge to me. Years later, while serving patrons remotely through digital reference, many of those principles still apply. Through the Web we have put a user-friendly face on the collections and services that librarians have been offering for hundreds of years. I hope that this book will help to strengthen and expand that tradition.

ONE

Planning Your Web Site

WHY PLANNING IS SO IMPORTANT

Planning for web site development is critical in building and maintaining a sustainable and scalable web site. The planning process helps managers determine the goals and priorities of the web site, which ultimately aids the web designer in the site's design and structure. Library web sites have enterprise-wide implications, and managers soon realize that upgrades to the site affect many staff members in addition to the customers the site serves. For example, the addition of electronic books (e-books) requires the collection development department to select the titles, technical services to load the MARC records into the catalog, the marketing department to create promotional materials, the information technology department to create authentication for remote use, and staff and public trainers to educate users. Of course, the selection of an e-books vendor, format, delivery, and the allocation of funds would have to precede all of these. Managers must realize that the more staff and departments they rely on to assist in web site development, the longer the process takes; however, each one is now a stakeholder in the process.

Written goals and objectives help the web manager determine and secure the resources necessary to accomplish these goals. Budgetary considerations include staffing, consulting fees, software, and hardware necessary to create and maintain the web site. The web site serves as a portal for customers to access collections and services of the library that must also be budgeted for. Additionally, marketing materials promoting the web site address and its

1

contents and services should be considered. When all is said and done, the library's web site may represent a substantial investment, in both financial and human resources.

The library web site is not only an entity unto itself with its own goals, but it can also be an instrumental part of helping other library departments achieve their goals. This may include supporting the goals of the collection development department, for example, in increasing the circulation of seldom-used materials or advertising the multilingual materials recently added to the collection.

SITE DEVELOPMENT PROCESS

Initially, one person in the library is responsible for beginning the site development process. This is normally a senior staff member who begins to organize staff, either through a committee or a point person; however, all libraries must review the site development process. Lynch and Horton state that a complex web site generally follows six major stages: site definition and planning, information architecture, site design, site construction, site marketing, and tracking, evaluation, and maintenance (Lynch and Horton 2002).

Site definition and planning include defining the goals and objectives of the web site. Included are not only content and services called for within the library's strategic plan, but also the resources needed to create and maintain them. The site definition and planning phase identifies staff roles, technology, and budgetary concerns.

Developing the information architecture of the web site includes creating an inventory of site content in the form of an outline, table of contents, or site map. Identify programming needs to support various features of the web site—such as the inclusion of an events database, virtual tour, or web tutorial—that may require the skills of a contractor or time allocated from staff within the library's technology department. Several prototypes representing alternative designs should be loosely created. "The key to good prototyping is flexibility early on; the site prototypes should not be so complex or elaborate that the team becomes too invested in one design at the expense of exploring better alternatives" (Lynch and Horton 2002, 8).

Site design includes creating content (texts and graphics), functionality (forms, surveys, search engine), a navigation bar, and templates. Templates assist web designers in maintaining consistency; the template is simply a web page that includes all of the materials that you want on each page within the site. Once the content for the web pages is produced, it is used to populate the templates, and the site is ultimately constructed.

Final editing, proofreading, and testing of the site begin. The web site address should be printed on all advertisements and marketing material, and a plan incorporating web marketing strategies should be created. This plan may include a listing in search engines; however, more importantly, the library should look to its community partners for reciprocal linking. The last stage of web site development includes tracking usage, evaluation, and maintenance of the site. Statistical tracking software will assist in identifying how the site is used. Web managers should build a process to determine pages that will need to be regularly updated, create a system for adding new content, and allow time for usability testing.

STAFFING MODEL

Staff members may be dedicated to the web site (web designer), or part of their duties may involve the web site (network administrator). In smaller organizations, there may be only one person in charge of the web site, creating content, making corrections, and, many times, serving on the public service desk. Staff involvement in web site responsibilities depends on job position, size of the organization, and goals of the web site.

Based on budget constraints, skill sets, and the size of the library, a combination of staffing models may work best. The skills necessary to build and maintain a library web site include art and design, programming and functionality, writing and editing, and management of all of the library's online activities, including vendor relations. Libraries have found that web site creation and maintenance demands the skills of *many* people in the organization.

A staff member with an enterprise-wide knowledge of the library's mission and strategy should manage the library web site. Libraries that have a successful online presence realize that the web site encompasses all aspects of its organization. Many libraries create a web advisory or web implementation committee that can direct the work of the web designer. Creating a web page can be easily done in any of the many web editors available; however, web site management encompasses not just the marking up of pages, but also the management of a complex web site. Web managers need to be familiar with web architecture principles, standards, and issues. They must be good project managers often consulting with staff throughout the organization. Web editorial and style guidelines must be established to maintain consistency among the various content creators. Web managers must also use site management and assessment tools. In addition to web designers and web librarians, staff are typically assigned certain aspects of web site responsibilities through committees, some of which may dissolve shortly after the initial web site is complete or a redesign of the web site is published. Vaughan describes staffing at the University of Nevada, Las Vegas (UNLV), libraries: "The overall web site planning and content issues are formulated by the web team, while many of the design issues and maintenance tasks are carried out by the technical services web developers. Library systems staff are responsible for such issues as script management, hardware management, statistics gathering, and backups" (2001, 83). Additionally, Vaughan states that each redesign of the UNLV web site has used a team-based approach, the first of which included six individuals from various areas (public services, technical services, and a branch librarian) and the library web administrator. Depending on the needs of the library, these groups have a wide range of duties such as content creation, site maintenance, design, usability and accessibility testing, and marketing.

In summer 2001, the Association of Research Libraries surveyed its 122 member libraries about staffing models for library web sites. The sixty-two libraries that responded to the survey revealed that "responsibility for web site content—developing, editing, revising, and updating—is widely distributed among staff. Reference librarians at nearly every responding library do this work (98 percent). Other positions that work with content are the library's web team (81 percent), collection development staff (81 percent), bibliographers (79 percent), and the webmaster (66 percent)" (Association of Research Libraries 2001).

Libraries also develop a centralized or decentralized model for web site maintenance, which has implications for the allocation of staff. Centralized models route content to one person, in most cases, the web designer. Decentralized models allow various departments to upload their information directly to the web server. Figure 1.1 displays an example of a calendar of events created using Active Server Pages (ASP) and a database to automate the updating process. A decentralized model without the use of guidelines, standards, or templates will eventually fail. The web site may experience inconsistency in presentation and navigation, outdated and incorrect information, and gaps in content, and its web pages may be noncompliant in usability and accessibility design so much so that users simply cannot find information (McConnell and Middleton 2002).

Klein suggests that 90 percent of the web content remains the same, but it is the remaining 10 percent that creates the largest burden of maintenance (2003, 28). In addition, it is this 10 percent that, for the most part, is tedious but necessary. These updates are clerical in nature and not related to the design or functionality of the web site. Klein's solution is to identify areas of the web site

Figure 1.1 Calendar of Events, Minneapolis (Minn.) Public Library

that need regular updates and the technology that can automate the updating process. For example, some items that change frequently on a library web site include programs and events. A database solution can offer a distributed way for staff to update their own content in this area. Klein's lesson makes sense: "Don't manage other people's information. Let them manage it themselves." The greater the opportunity for staff to upload to the web site, within standards and guidelines in the form of a template or database entry form, the more time the web developer has to devote to other projects. It is important to consider whether a job description is flexible enough to accommodate the new duties or whether it needs to be rewritten (Mach and Kutzik 2001). If templates or database entry forms are created, however, updates become a matter of data entry, which do not require knowledge of HyperText Markup Language (HTML) or web editing software. "Developing and maintaining a simple web page could move from a highly specialized skill for a few individuals to an ordinary task for many" (31). For more information about database-driven library applications, *see High Tech, High Touch: Library Customer Service through Technology*, by Lynn Jurewicz and Todd Cutler (ALA, Chicago, 2003).

Clearly, the web site is everyone's responsibility, and each library must allocate key staff to its creation and maintenance. Web site statistics, including the amount of online renewals and the number of requests placed, are indicative of usage. Web site usage will generally continue to rise as technology improves access to online databases and library catalogs become more customer-oriented. Remote usage will rise exponentially faster than in-house usage because the number of computers, or access points, are limitless outside of the library. With the increase in the amount of resources available online, many libraries have created positions that reflect this trend, such as web librarian, electronic resource librarian, and other variations of job titles. In addition to overall web site management, staff members in these positions are generally responsible for online databases (collections) and electronic reference (services).

Because web site creation includes so many varied tasks, the responsibility must be distributed. It would be impossible to find all of the necessary skills in one staff member. It is incumbent upon library administration to recognize this and ensure that sufficient staffing models exist to harness talent within its staff.

LIBRARY PLANNING DOCUMENTS

Planning documents chart the course for future services and outline how the organization is going to achieve its goals and objectives. The goals of the web site should complement, support, and work in tandem with existing planning documents and policies. In addition to the implementation of these goals, the web site also is an appropriate place to publish them. Placement of planning documents and policies, both pertaining to the library and the library's web site, should typically be placed under the section titled, About the Library, as displayed in figure 1.2.

Strategic and Action Plans

Strategic plans normally direct the course of action for the organization over several years. Action plans offer more details on how the library is going to accomplish its goals. Scan through these documents and create a list of where the library web site is called upon to help achieve certain objectives or where the web site can actually implement online activities in support of strategic initiatives. Again, the web site also offers a way to publish strategic plans and provide progress reports to the community. For example, the General Library at the University of Texas at Austin displays the strategic plan in PDF and status reports. (*See* figure 1.3.)

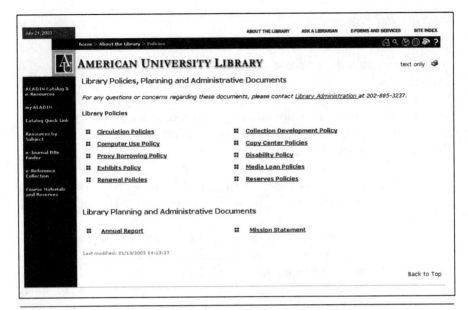

Figure 1.2 Policies Displayed in About the Library, American University Library (Washington, D.C.)

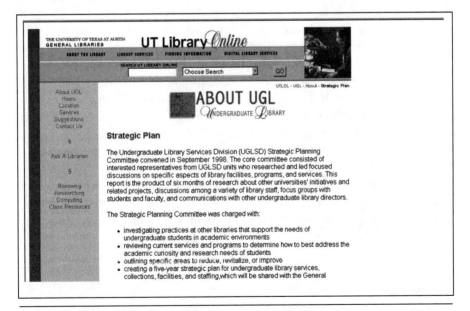

Figure 1.3 Strategic Plan, University of Texas at Austin. The library's strategic plan and progress report is posted at About the Library.

Policies and Procedures

Libraries create a great deal of policies that guide library staff in daily operations. These public documents also have implications for the library web site. For example, the library's policy on patron confidentiality has an impact on the way patrons log on to their accounts and send personal information to the library via forms and e-mail. In addition, the circulation policy should be reviewed when planning the services patrons will be able to access via the web site. Services patrons are able to access over the Internet should not circumvent existing policies, such as limits on renewals or the number of requests or holds patrons are allowed. Other policies that should be reviewed before planning services for the web site include borrowing, interlibrary loan, and collection development.

In *Library Web Site Policies*, Traw writes, "This constant demand and workload leave little time for a sole administrator or web team to prepare policies that give web sites direction and that establish roles and responsibilities of participants in the production process" (2000, 1). It is important that policy documents be created because they lay the foundation for direction and define responsibilities. Libraries are typically proactive in creating policy documents that will stand up to patron and board scrutiny when, and if, the need arises. However, it is usually at that time of need that a library finds that its documents need updating or it questions parts of the policy and determines it needs to be revised. Libraries should not wait for a problem to arise to create or revise existing web site policies but rather schedule an annual review of such policies. For the most part, these policies are public documents and are freely available on the Web for viewing. In fact, there are many sources for libraries to help them craft legal documents on their own or as a draft to hand to their legal counsel.

Libraries may also produce web site policies that aid in the creation and management of the web site. The most commonly included procedural and technical elements are submission and contribution procedures, spell checking and proofreading for errors, testing pages prior to uploading, web browser compliance, and server access (Traw 2000). Traw's research indicates that policies more administrative in nature were also identified as important and include site responsibilities, web site mission, target audience, scope of the site, and administrative structure.

Disclaimers

Disclaimers are the equivalent of the "small print" stating that the library will not be held liable for the information it displays on its web site including linking to external sites. Below is an excerpt from the disclaimer used at the University of Wisconsin Law Library (2002):

> The UW makes no representations or warranties of any kind regarding the information contained on this site. This site may contain links to web pages outside of the UW Law Library domain, for which no copyright interest is claimed nor responsibility assumed. Internet links are limited to those that meet the essential mission of the UW Law Library.

Linking to External Web Sites

Linking to external sites poses many challenges for libraries. What may seem to be a simple request for adding a link to a public web site can cause problems when no linking policy exists. When denied a link from the city web site, Geoffrey Davidian, publisher of the *Putnam Pit*, an alternative newspaper, claimed that his First Amendment rights were violated, and he filed a lawsuit against the City of Cookeville (Tenn.) (Kennedy 2000). When the lower court found for the city, Davidian appealed, and it was in the Sixth Circuit Court that the city was basically found vulnerable to a charge of First Amendment violations (Latham 2002).

"As libraries develop a stronger and more robust Web presence, as they attract greater numbers of users, and as they expend professional time and energy in expanding access, the need for a link collection policy becomes apparent, even without legal challenges" (Latham 2002, 21). The library is, politically, a good association for just about anybody, and as Latham describes, when people realize the potential reach of a library's web site, more and more requests for links may increase a library's exposure to liability. Furthermore, libraries should not allow patrons to submit suggestions for links, however appropriate they may be, because this may give the impression that the library's web site is a public forum, which it is not. (For more information, *see* chapter 5.)

Privacy Policies

A privacy policy states to visitors the type of information collected and how it is acquired, used, stored, and kept secure in brief nonlegalese, nontechnical terminology. A privacy policy is essential because many visitors, before creating accounts or submitting personal information via a form, may question the security of their information. Visitors should have the option of reading the privacy statement each time they are asked to provide personal information such as when filling out interlibrary loan forms, entering contests, e-mailing reference questions, or applying for a library card. Some libraries may include online privacy statements separately or may include them in the library's general statement on privacy. Legislation, such as the USA Patriot Act, may affect the extent to which a library can protect the privacy of its customers. The Office of Intellectual Freedom of the American Library Association often issues updates regarding how legislation may affect libraries.

Often patrons look for privacy policies when they are asked to type in personally identifiable information such as library card numbers, phone numbers, or their names and addresses. The following list is based on *How to Read a Privacy Policy*; your policy should address the following nine concerns (Center for Democracy and Technology 2001).

1. Explain the collection of personal identifiable information.
2. Explain the rationale behind collecting information.
3. Describe the type of technology used to collect data. Does the site set cookies or maintain weblogs?
4. Explain how personal information is used once it is collected.
5. Explain the availability of privacy preferences, if any, such as turning off cookies. Will the user still be able to use all of the site's functionality?
6. Can users access information that has been collected about them? Are users able to correct inaccurate data?
7. Let visitors know how long personal information is stored.
8. Explain the complaint and redress process. Whom can users contact?
9. Explain if any laws impact the privacy of stored personal information.

For more information

COPPA: Important Policy Notice to Libraries on Children's Online Privacy
    http://www.ala.org, search COPPA
    Contains several documents that discuss COPPA and libraries.

DMA's Privacy Policy Generator
    http://www.the-dma.org/privacy/privacypolicygenerator.shtml
    Allows users to create dynamic privacy policies by filling out a form.

CONTENT INVENTORY

Although many libraries already have an online presence, eventually libraries will undertake a redesign of their web sites. Libraries can begin by combing through the existing web site and listing all of the items to be included on the new web site. Make note of areas that simply describe services rather than offer them online. These may serve as potential online services for future versions of the web site. For example, if the library offers computer usage, perhaps in the future visitors may reserve computers via the library web site.

This content inventory list should include services and collections available in the physical buildings and online. Also include existing content, if you are planning a site redesign, as well as information about the library as an organization. This list will help you create a site index and navigation menus. Figure 1.4 provides a checklist, which is also available on this book's companion web site (http://www.webliography.org). This checklist can be used during the final review process to make sure that all of the content is included in the final version.

STYLE GUIDES AND STANDARDS

Style guides define specifications for web authors and include a blend of technical standards, rules of design, and editorial guidelines. They ensure consistency and clarity as users visit pages throughout the web site—pages that may be authored by different content creators. Many style guides exist; however, librarians may find it necessary to supplement these with a style guide to cover local concerns. In fact, an existing style guide the library uses for print documents may be a starting point. The guide may address local spelling or expression of places and locations. The style guide should include a list of referring documents such as a writing guide, grammar book, and dictionary. Libraries must take into consideration their audience (accessibility issues, speed connections, browser usage) when creating their style guides. Listed below are some items that should be included in your style guide. Some libraries create templates, Cascading Style Sheets (CSS), and images for staff so that they can merely place the content in a shell and it has the look and feel of the library's main site. For a listing of web style guides, *see* appendix B.

If the library web site was created by an outside agency, ask for a copy of their style guide so when the library begins maintaining its web site, the style remains consistent. When multiple staff members participate in updating the web site through databases or content management software, style guides ensure that data input on their end display consistently as output on the web page.

Technology

Defining and documenting the technology used on a web site ensures consistency, ultimately makes use of existing resources, and is cost-effective. Webmasters

Use the checklist to help gather information. List the contact person, date promised, and the status (received).

☐ account information	☐ fees and fines	☐ meeting room
☐ annual reports	☐ films	☐ microfiche readers
☐ names of board of trustees	☐ forms	☐ mission statement
☐ book discussion groups	☐ foundation	☐ organizational chart
☐ books	☐ friends of the library	☐ planning documents
☐ borrowing materials	☐ gallery exhibits	☐ policies
☐ cards	☐ GED classes	☐ reference services
☐ children's programs	☐ government documents	☐ renew materials
☐ classes	☐ history of the library	☐ request materials
☐ computer use	☐ homebound services	☐ research assistance
☐ contact information	☐ homework help	☐ reserves
☐ copy machines	☐ hours of operation	☐ school visits
☐ course reserves	☐ instruction	☐ special collections
☐ department and staff directory	☐ interlibrary loan	☐ staff directory
☐ disability services	☐ Internet access	☐ story time
☐ document delivery	☐ journals and indexes	☐ study rooms
☐ donations	☐ laptop checkout	☐ book suggestions
☐ e-books	☐ library card	☐ tours of the library
☐ e-mail reference	☐ library director	☐ tutoring and proctoring services
☐ employment	☐ library programs	☐ used books
☐ ESL classes	☐ links to other sites	☐ volunteers
☐ events	☐ literacy	
☐ exhibits	☐ locations: maps, driving directions, parking	
☐ faculty services	☐ magazines and newspapers	
☐ fax machines		

Figure 1.4   Content Inventory Checklist

should consult the World Wide Web Consortium (W3C) for current web standards (http://www.w3c.org). The W3C develops and promotes standard technologies such as HTML, Extensible Markup Language (XML), and CSS. When publishing web sites using current standards, libraries ensure that their sites will be accessible by the majority of their users regardless of browser or platform. Using the most current standards can also reduce the cost of web site production and provides significant savings when redesigning a web site (Bickner 2002).

Browser Requirements and Plug-Ins

Nielsen lists three reasons to be conservative when embracing web innovations such as plug-ins and browser-specific features: (1) with an upgrade speed of about 1 percent per week, it will be a year before the majority of users will even be able to access it; (2) even after the new technology moves from beta status, there will probably be some bugs in it; and (3) the best ways of using a new web technology come about after a lot of trial and error (Nielsen 2000). Nielsen suggests letting somebody else make those mistakes. Bickner maintains that web browsers experienced a shift from proprietary rendering to standards-based rendering, and that up through the 4.0 browsers, Netscape and Internet Explorer displayed web pages differently as each browser interpreted markup tags by their own definitions (Bickner 2002).

Because the library web site also connects to subscription databases and the catalog, the creation of which is out of the control of the library's webmaster, it is critical to survey vendor web sites and document minimum browser requirements and plug-ins necessary to search, access, and view their materials.

Example

Hillsborough County (Fla.) Public Library Cooperative
   http://www.hcplc.org/hcplc/tech

   This cooperative maintains a web page on their site titled Help, which outlines the suggested specifications for optimum access to resources on their web site as well as third-party vendors.

Testing Pages

Testing pages before making them live is critical in providing accurate information to users. Broken links and spelling errors erode the trust of visitors to the web site. Libraries should also determine the browsers and operating systems they will choose to support. Most web site statistics programs will capture this type of information, which gives webmasters a good idea of the number of visitors coming to the site using certain browsers and operating systems. Free tools are available that check spelling, external links, image size, and HTML tags. (*See* appendix B.)

CSS (Cascading Style Sheets)

CSS allow you to assign certain design specifications to a group of documents. The appealing part of style sheets in web design is the ability to change the look of many documents at once without having to touch every page. CSS are similar to the style sheets found in word-processing software. If you have marked certain categories as headings, you can change the look of all headings by altering the style of that heading.

CSS offer web designers two key advantages in managing complex web sites (Lynch and Horton 2002, 118):

> *Separation of content and design.* CSS give site developers the best of both worlds: content markup that reflects the logical structure of the information and the freedom to specify exactly how each HTML tag will look.

> *Efficient control over large document sets.* The most powerful implementations of CSS will allow site designers to control the graphic "look and feel" of thousands of pages by modifying a single master style sheet document.

For more information

Cascading Style Sheets (Web Design Group)
http://www.htmlhelp.com/reference/css

Cascading Style Sheets (World Wide Web Consortium)
http://www.w3.org/Style/CSS

Word and Phrase List

Libraries should continue to keep track of certain terms and phrases that have the potential to be misspelled or used incorrectly. The list should be updated and accessible to anyone who writes content for library publications. Many times content from a print publication is copied to the web site. A list of acceptable words and phrases sends a consistent and clear message to readers.

desktop

disk (floppy disk)

download

e-mail

home page

interlibrary loan

Internet

library catalog, not web catalog

Library District

Macintosh

menu-driven

multimedia

offline

online

PIN not PIN number

place a request or request an item, material (not reserve)

plug-in

research databases

research tools (not online tools)

screensaver

spell checker

Userid

Web

web page

web site

Time and Date Expressions
5 P.M.

1/14 • 9:30 A.M. - 1 P.M.

12 noon

January 30, 2003 • 9:00 A.M.
      (as displayed from results of events database search)

Titles
Italicize titles of books, magazines, and videos.

Include links to the catalog.

Editorial Calendar

Creating content for a web site is challenging; however, maintaining that information and creating new, timely information for the home page is becoming increasingly difficult to manage. An editorial calendar can assist in managing the web developer's work flow by outlining content submissions and deadlines and deleting content. An editorial calendar will assist in planning for content based on events. Each listing should include the contact name of the person responsible for content, submission deadlines, review period, publication date, and the date to pull the pages off of the web site. It may also be helpful to identify the pages that the content will appear on (home page, secondary pages, etc.). Calendars should also include dates the library will be closed. Appendix A provides a sample calendar.

HOUSEKEEPING AND "OTHER DUTIES AS REQUIRED"

Web managers must deal with a number of maintenance issues on a continual basis. Some of these are certainly mundane and quite tedious; however, they usually fall to the responsibility of the web staff because these staff members are closest to the information or the process where updating is carried out. Maintenance tasks include link checking, backing up the web site, and gathering usage statistics.

Link Checking

Finding, organizing, and maintaining links to external web sites consumes a great deal of time. Free link checkers will test access to external links by detecting bad connections or redirects; however, redirects may indicate a change in authoring agency. The links must always be checked manually to determine if the content of the page has changed and if the content still falls under the library's selection criteria. For a list of link checkers, *see* appendix B.

For more information

World Wide Web Consortium Link Checker
   http://validator.w3.org/checklink
      This web page allows you to enter a URL and it will check for dead links.

Backing Up the Web Site

Creating and saving copies of the files that make up the web site at another location provides a "backup copy" should something happen to the production or live server. Backing up your web site provides you with a last known good copy of the site. If you lose files or overwrite them accidentally, or make a change that just does not work, you can revert back to the saved files. Archiving the contents of a web site demands a much more deliberate and planned process. Libraries scan text, photos, images, and create online libraries backed by objects stored in databases. Content that is part of a digital library such as local images should be preserved in a nonproprietary format. Because the files are not compressed, they tend to be larger, so server space may be a consideration depending on the size of the collection. A procedure for preserving this content should be created and followed.

The frequency of copying the web site to another location depends on how often the site is updated. In most cases, the server backs up the files on a nightly basis, but it is much more convenient to have a copy located on a CD-ROM so that you can quickly access previous versions of the web site. If an Internet service provider hosts the web site, inquire how frequently the site is backed up and if the backup files are accessible to library staff. There are other reasons to back up the web site, such as recycling previously used graphics and web pages. If your library celebrates annual events, then you can take previously used content and update it with new information. The library may also need to use screen shots of earlier web pages for marketing purposes.

Gathering Usage Statistics

As libraries increase their amount of electronic resources and more locally produced content is accessible through the Web, they must find meaningful ways to measure their usage. Much of patrons' library business can now be done remotely. For instance, patrons can retrieve a list of the items they have checked out, materials they have on request, and a summary of fees and fines. They can also request items, cancel holds, and renew books. An increase in the usage of licensed databases may be the reason for a decline in reference statistics. However, real-time chat reference may attract a new user group and consequently increase reference statistics. Accuracy in compiling data is important because the numbers have implications not only for collection development, but also for budgetary concerns, training issues, and marketing efforts.

Although significant improvement has been made over the last few years in streamlining reporting practices of licensed database vendors, the reporting methods still vary. Vendor reports are generated a variety of ways and come in different formats. The more advanced systems allow librarians to enter an administrative web page, normally with a user name and password, and generate the reports with configurable time ranges and file formats. They also have automatic e-mail reporting to any number of staff members. Less advanced systems e-mail librarians several days into the new month, some even toward the middle of the month, or deliver statistics via fax. Normally, most vendors report monthly; however, some may issue daily or quarterly reports. Figures on the following transactions are generally available: log-ins or sessions, searches, pages viewed (citations, abstracts, and full text), and number of articles or records downloaded or e-mailed.

In addition, statistics may be generated that are specific to each database. Librarians can be notified if the number of simultaneous users exceeds the limit set out in the contract. They will know how many of their users were bumped or unable to use the product. Additionally, e-books allow one simultaneous user per copy, so reports display any titles that were locked out to patrons at any one time.

As an increasing amount of money is budgeted for online materials, administrators want to ensure that the money is well spent and usage continues to rise. Studies and guidelines have emerged from librarians, consortia, and several organizations listed below. In response to librarian demand, Release 1 of the COUNTER Code of Practice focuses on the usage of journals and databases, the products that account for the largest share of most libraries' materials budgets (COUNTER 2002). Note that the "turnaway" report is applicable only where the user access model is based on a maximum number of concurrent users.

Level 1 compliancy requires the following:

> *Journal Report 1:* Number of successful full-text article requests by month and journal
>
> *Journal Report 2:* Turnaways by month and journal
>
> *Database Report 1:* Total searches and sessions by month and database
>
> *Database Report 2:* Turnaways by month and database
>
> *Database Report 3:* Total searches and sessions by month and service

Level 2 compliancy requires the following:

> *Journal Report 3:* Number of successful item requests and turnaways by month, journal, and page type
>
> *Journal Report 4:* Total searches run by month and service (includes saved searches, modified searches, and searches with zero results)

Organizations involved in setting standards for usage statistics follow:

> ARL New Measures Initiative
> http://www.arl.org/stats/newmeas/newmeas.html
>
> This effort represents the academic community's response to an increasing demand for libraries to demonstrate outcomes and effects in areas important to the institution and the increasing pressure to maximize the use of resources.

COUNTER (Counting Online Usage of Networked Electronic Resources)
http://www.projectcounter.org

Established in March 2002, COUNTER published the *COUNTER Code of Practice,* which provides guidance on data elements to be measured, definitions of these data elements, and output report content and format.

The International Coalition of Library Consortia (ICOLC)
http://www.library.yale.edu/consortia/2001webstats.htm

ICOLC represents 150 library consortia worldwide. Their publication, *Guidelines for Statistical Measures of Usage of Web-Based Information Resources,* was modified in December 2001 to simplify data and strengthen administrative concerns such as confidentiality, privacy, access, delivery, and report format.

National Information Standards Organization (NISO)
http://www.niso.org

The Library Statistics Standard, ANSI/NISO Z39.7-1995, was first released in 1968 and revised in 1983 and 1995. Revisions currently in development will incorporate electronic usage statistics and performance measures.

Despite tremendous improvement in the standardization of the type of data collected, the data collection process continues to be time-consuming and cumbersome. Several factors are at play, such as the number of databases from each vendor and the number of vendors as well as the delivery method: e-mail, fax, or web site. When the numbers are retrieved, they must be placed into a spreadsheet so that they have meaning and can tell a story. When standards are more formalized, perhaps software solutions will streamline this process; however, some resource integration software (*see* chapter 6) may have the capabilities to accomplish this task.

Measuring success within the library profession has traditionally been based on numbers and transactions: how many items circulated, reference questions answered, interlibrary loans filled, Internet sign-ups, and renewals. Additionally, we count the number of students at workshops, children at a story time, and hours we are open to the public. Gathering statistics for networked resources has challenged libraries to determine the value of these numbers and how they can be used effectively. Usage statistics tell us how many sessions or downloads were recorded, but is it possible to really know if our users are finding relevancy in the items they are retrieving? If the numbers cannot give us subjective information, they can certainly guide us in the evaluation and development of the online collection as well as training opportunities that may have otherwise not been known.

Libraries can use statistics to determine whether to renew or discontinue the subscription to a product. Additionally, statistics derived from certain databases can illustrate the need for complementary information in that subject or genre. For example, if the monthly report shows that the most frequently checked out e-books are computer books, then perhaps the library should purchase access to more titles or more simultaneous licenses to existing titles (more copies). Electronic usage may also have implications for the print collection. It may be determined that the information is easier to access in electronic format than in paper. Some libraries comb through print journal subscriptions to determine if online access is available and, if so, preferable.

Usage statistics can also help identify parts of the online collection that may be underutilized because staff members and library users do not know that they exist, the database may be difficult to use, or it is not presented well on the web site. For example, high or low usage for some databases can simply mean that they are either the first or the last database listed on the page. Library trainers should have access to monthly statistics so they are aware of the database usage and can plan training or promotional materials for their advertising.

Database usage tracked monthly over a period of months, or years, can indicate the level of usage. Spikes and dips may appear during summer break and holiday vacations, and usage may spike shortly after training sessions or library orientations. The comparison between internal and remote access should also be considered, as external usage will most certainly outpace usage from within the library. Statistics can tell many different stories. Fortunately, industry experts are currently formulating statistical reporting standards so that the reporting remains consistent and the numbers can be used to make critical decisions regarding resource allocation.

TWO

Information Architecture

nformation architecture provides the infrastructure for information systems. It involves organizing, structuring, labeling, retrieving, and managing information. Many of these concepts already exist in libraries. Take, for instance, the library catalog. It contains a MARC record for each piece of material owned by the library. A certain taxonomy is used to categorize each item. The catalog has a retrieval mechanism that outputs results in a chronological, numerical, or alphabetical order. Librarians are already familiar with the organization of information within information systems, both online and in print. The Web offers further challenges for libraries including design, usability, and accessibility.

As defined in *Information Architecture for the World Wide Web* (Rosenfeld and Morville 2002, 4), information architecture is

1. the combination of organization, labeling, and navigation schemes within an information system;
2. the structural design of an information space to facilitate task completion and intuitive access to content;
3. the art and science of structuring and classifying web sites and intranets to help people find and manage information; and
4. an emerging discipline and community of practice focused on bringing principles of design and architecture to the digital landscape.

Once web site goals are established and libraries determine the content and services they are going to deliver online, it is time to begin designing the structure of the site. This includes how each page will interact within the structure of the site. In addition, plan for change. Determine future collections or services the library may offer and where they would fit in to the existing structure. For example, if a library knows that it will be creating a digital collection of local images with a go-live date two years in the future, think about where it would fit best in the current structure. Scalable web sites, that is, those that are built for change, provide the best weapon against fragmented web sites, which do not adapt well to shifting services and collections and are difficult to update.

Site architecture should reflect users' needs and not the organizational structure of the library. Libraries typically have a difficult time separating tasks from their associated departments just as visitors do when deciphering which department can best serve them. User-centered labels favor focusing on tasks rather than library department names (e.g., "learn to read" versus "literacy"). Task-oriented labels are appropriate when it is possible to anticipate a limited number of high-priority tasks visitors will want to accomplish (Rosenfeld and Morville 2002). For instance, patrons perform the following popular tasks: renew materials, view account status, request a book, and find a magazine article.

The design will take on a different arrangement depending on the characteristics of the information. Exact organization schemes are "relatively easy to design and maintain because there is little intellectual work involved in assigning items to categories" (Rosenfeld and Morville 2002, 56). Pages can be arranged alphabetically (e.g., site index), chronologically (e.g., board of trustee minutes), geographically (e.g., branch locations), topically (e.g., bibliographies), or by format (e.g., circulating materials), audience (e.g., kid's page), and task (e.g., renew materials).

SITE NAVIGATION

Web site navigation includes the main navigation bar, site maps, site indexes, and a search function. Most importantly, taxonomy is critical when creating a usable web site. Users need meaningful labels so that they are able to associate their meanings with the content for which they came. Besides the main navigation bar, visitors may also find information on the web site by entering text into a site's search feature or by browsing the site map. In addition to creating useful content, visitors must be able to find it. One of the most frequent mistakes libraries make when creating web sites for their customers is that they forget about the user. The underlying goal of all web sites is to create a user-centered design that allows users to easily navigate, locate materials, and inter-act with each page.

Library web sites are typically content-rich and contain a wide variety of information and services; therefore, if the site is large enough, both a site map and site index would be appropriate. It is also important to accommodate the different ways that people look for information. Some visitors prefer to browse, while others would rather type their terms into the search box and hope the results bring them to their destination. Usability studies show that slightly more than half of all the users are search-dominant, about a fifth of the users are link-dominant, and the rest exhibit a combination of the two (Nielsen 2000).

Libraries struggle with terminology that will be meaningful to visitors familiar with library services as well as new users they are hoping to attract. For example, a common phrase in librarianship is "the Friends of the Library." For librarians, the Friends provide opportunities for people to volunteer and help support the library through fund-raising. Use of this phrase may be somewhat ambiguous to visitors unfamiliar with this organization. Perhaps phrases like "volunteer" or "donate" or "Support the Library" more appropriately convey the meaning of the content.

Labeling

Labeling sections or pages of your web site is critical for visitors to determine their destination. Labels must clearly identify content by using terms and phrases free of library jargon. Consider using the following terms as they are standard and familiar to most of your visitors (Rosenfeld and Morville 2002, 87):

- Home, Main, Main Page
- Search, Find, Browse, Search/Browse
- Site Map, Contents, Table of Contents, Index
- Contact, Contact Us
- Help, FAQ, Frequently Asked Questions
- News, News and Events, Announcements
- About, About Us, About <company name>, Who We Are

Because libraries typically serve different constituents, standardization is not necessary; however, use of terms that visitors are accustomed to has its advantages. Using those terms listed above will assist libraries in finding com-mon naming conventions that visitors will recognize. It is clear that libraries use a variety of terms to describe similar content and services offered among libraries. Several published usability studies have revealed the following best practices (Kupersmith 2003):

> Test to see what users understand. Use test data from other libraries whose user population resembles your own.
>
> Use "target words," such as *book* or *articles*, that correspond to the end product the user is seeking.
>
> Emphasize alternatives to the library catalog (e.g., Find Books).
>
> Enhance menu items with explanatory text or graphics or both using mouseovers or ALT tags [Mouseovers, created with Javascript, and ALT tags, found within HTML, are techniques used to offer visitors more information when they place their mouses over an image.]
>
> Provide glossaries of library terms or "What's this?" explanations of individual terms.
>
> Provide intermediate pages in cases where a top-level menu choice presents ambiguities that can't be resolved in the space available.
>
> Provide alternative paths in cases where users are likely to make predictable "wrong" choices.

Site Maps

A site map offers an overview of the web site and an alternative to the main navigation bar. Site maps provide an organizational chart showing main categories and the links within them (*see* figure 2.1). Visitors may click on any of the links and be taken to that page. In addition, if visitors have already viewed any of the pages listed in the site map, they will appear as a visited link. If designed well, this overview can include several levels of hierarchy and yet not be so big that users lose their ability to grasp the map as a whole (Nielsen 2002). Site maps can be generated within a web editor, such as FrontPage (Microsoft) and Dreamweaver (Macromedia), or created manually.

Site Indexes

A site index is similar to the back-of-the-book indexing to which librarians are accustomed. The index differs from a site map because it does not represent a hierarchy of the site's organization. It lists keywords, phrases, terms, and concepts that visitors may use. Site indexes are used when the users know what they are looking for but cannot find it in the main navigation bar and cannot determine which heading it may be classified under. Considerations for creating a

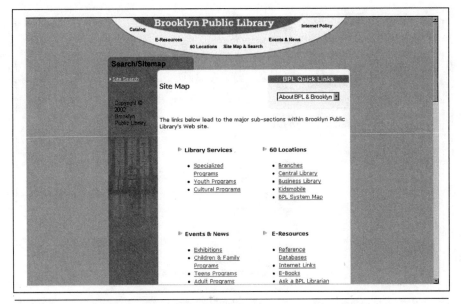

Figure 2.1   A Site Map on the Brooklyn (N.Y.) Public Library's Web Site
(http://www.brooklynpubliclibrary.org/search/sitemap.htm)

site index include determining the level of granularity, or how detailed the index will be; the permutation of terms and agreed-upon phrases and words to be used; and the process by which the index will be maintained. Libraries should try to anticipate users' queries when building the index and the variety of terms used to describe the content (e.g., classes, instruction, computers). Designers should seek input from public service staff because they experience firsthand what terms and phrases their customers use (*see* figure 2.2 for an example of a site index).

Site indexes enhance information access for obvious reasons, but several deterrents to their creation include cost, problems with updating, and the fact that many webmasters usually do not consider them in the planning phase (Browne 2001). Web sites that start out small may eventually grow to the point that they need a site index; however, planning for its creation should be initiated during preliminary stages of web site development. Additionally, Browne states that web site indexing requires skills just as back-of-the-book indexing does; indexers must have the ability to analyze the subject of documents, to describe that subject in its language, to consider alternative access points, and to create references to or from headings.

Figure 2.2 Site Index, University of Rhode Island Libraries
(http://www.uri.edu/library/siteindex.html)

For more information

Browne, Glenda, and Jonathan Jermey. 2001. *Web site indexing: Enhancing access to information within web sites*. South Australia: Auslib Press.

Rowland, Marilyn, and Diane Brenner, eds. 2000. *Beyond book indexing: How to get started in web indexing, embedded indexing, and other computer-based media*. Medford, N.J.: Information Today.

Site Search Function

Users may find they are lost or are looking for something so specific that a quick glance at the main navigation bar determines that searching the site is their best option. Users enter their text into the box and press ENTER. Most users are not aware of keyword, phrase, or Boolean searching. They simply enter their text and want to be directed to the correct page. Only when they do not find results in the first screen or two do they return to the help file for more specific information on how to construct their search string. Site search software can reside locally on the web server or can be hosted. Customizations of this feature can improve the results visitors retrieve. For example, certain directories that do not contain web content, like the cgi-bin directory, which contains scripts, should be blocked from the search. Web sites may also use a commercial search engine, like Google's SiteSearch, for free; however, libraries should check to see if the search engine sells advertisements on the results page, because such advertisements may not be appropriate for a library web site.

Search engines supplement manual indexes by offering access to more detailed information, finding topics with well-defined names and specific terms, and catering to those people with a preference for computer searching versus browsing (Browne 2001).

Because patrons in the building may be seeking links to search engines, many libraries, for purposes of convenience, allow visitors to choose between "Search This Site" or "Search the Web." However, industry experts say there is no need to clutter screens by offering a search engine feature that allows users to choose whether to search the current site or the entire Internet (Nielsen 2000). Most people know where to find a web-wide search engine because these sites are the most used services on the Web.

For more information

Rosenfeld, Louis, and Peter Morville. 2002. Search systems. In *Information architecture for the World Wide Web*. 2d ed. Sebastopol, Calif.: O'Reilly.

Library Portals and Customization

Library portals are changing rapidly, but four major components are common: (1) a single-search interface, (2) user authentication, (3) resource linking, and (4) content enhancement (Boss 2002). A single-search interface allows visitors to execute one search, which simultaneously retrieves results from research and periodical databases, including the library catalog. User authentication requires users to identify themselves, usually with a library card number. Resource linking provides a way for periodical databases to determine which database includes the full text of an article (rather than a citation or abstract). Last, content enhancement includes information that supplements bibliographic records in the catalog, such as cover art images, tables of contents, author notes, and more. Each of the four components listed above are treated in greater detail throughout this book.

Customization of special entry web pages is another consideration for libraries. Special entry pages include those created for use by library patrons who are physically in the library or certain departments within the library, staff members, and remote users. Kupersmith advises libraries to "start by establishing who will be using the page, what they need from it, and what knowledge they will likely bring to it" (Kupersmith 2003). Special entry web pages must also include certain elements required on the home page, such as the navigation bar and library logo. *See* chapter 8 for more information on web sites for specific audiences.

The Internet has brought an overwhelming amount of information directly to end users. Customized web pages offer information providers a way to help users access that information in a more useful and contextual way. Customized web pages offer visitors a customer-centered design where users actually choose the content displayed. Customization involves giving the user direct control over some combination of presentation, navigation, and content options (Rosenfeld and Morville 2002). Some libraries offering the customization of their web pages use MyLibrary, an open source software that allows customers to choose what information they see on their page after they log in to their accounts.

For example, in most cases, users can display a link to the librarian, links within the university, links to specific databases and electronic journals, and links to web sites. Once displayed, the screen gives the user the option to edit by either adding or deleting data to the category. Users can toggle buttons on and off when they want to revise their profiles.

Questions libraries may need to answer before considering creating a customizable portal page follow:

> Will the amount of usage justify the cost and time of creating a customized access point to library collections and services?

> How will the page be updated? Will library staff be feeding information into a database that provides current information for users?

> Can access to the user's library account be incorporated into authentication of proprietary databases without having to type further user names or library card numbers?

Examples

Brarydog, Public Library of Charlotte and Mecklenburg County (N.C.)
http://www.brarydog.net

North Carolina State University
http://my.lib.ncsu.edu

University of Washington
http://www.lib.washington.edu

Virginia Commonwealth University
http://www.library.vcu.edu/mylibrary

For more information

Boss, Richard W. 2002. Library web portals. Available at http://www.ala.org; search *library web portals.*

Local Systems and Services Committee, MARS. 1999. *Personalized library services: Innovative web-based reference services: A selected list.* Available at http://www.ala.org.

Morgan, Eric Lease. 2003. MyLibrary. Available at http://dewey.library.nd.edu/mylibrary.

Morgan, Eric Lease, ed. 2000. Special issue: User-customizable library portals. *Information Technology and Libraries* 19, no. 4 (December).

USABILITY

The concept of information architecture also incorporates design principles that cater to the needs of visitors. The information architect, or the person who designs the site's structure, keeps notes about what might be confusing and designs prototypes specifically for user testing to isolate issues in navigation, process, and understandability (Kimen 1999). User-centered design (UCD) was listed as one of the top technology issues facing today's libraries (LITA 2002). The UCD process starts with a multidisciplinary UCD project team who will

identify the target audience;

recruit members of the target audience as testers;

study the competition, including any other means the target audience uses to accomplish the task;

create a prototype based on users' task requirements;

have participants test the prototype;

develop a beta version based on the performance, reactions, and comments about the prototype;

release the product with a mechanism for customer feedback in place for future improvements (IBM).

Libraries should employ the conventions and standards evolved through web development that users are familiar with. Web surfers spend much time visiting other web sites in between trips to the library's site and become accustomed to generally accepted web design principles (Nielsen and Tahir 2002).

Users expect to find those same practices implemented on the library web site. Imagine all of the other sites (eBay, Travelocity, Yahoo!) that users visit in between trips to the library's web page. Using unconventional methods to access content and services will alienate many users. In fact, studying the design of some of the very heavily visited web sites helps libraries in adopting some of the very principles that makes these sites popular. Libraries should strive to be unique in the content they provide, not in their design conventions.

Navigation

Providing even the most relevant content is going to do visitors no good without proper navigational cues so that patrons can easily find information and maneuver through the site. Visitors should always have a clear understanding of where they are in the site, what pages they have visited, and what options are available for continued navigation. As discussed previously, some users like to browse and some like to search. When visitors use the site's search function, they are presented with their results ranked by relevancy and listed by page title. Clearly titled web pages assist searchers by providing cues to the content of their results. Additionally, designers can assist browsers by making no destination more than three clicks away from the home page.

File Size and Response Times

Web site visitors will not tolerate excessive periods of time waiting for pages to load into their browsers. A one-second response time is required for users to feel they are moving through the site uninhibited, while no more than a ten-second wait keeps user's attention on the task (Nielsen 2000).

Several factors determine the response time users experience while visiting the web site. The response time is affected by the total sum of all of the files embedded into the web page, including the file size of the page itself, the speed of the computer, the user's connection to the Internet (modem dial-up, cable modem, T-1 line), and server and Internet traffic. Figure 2.3 illustrates the average response time for specific file sizes based on the speed of the user's Internet connection.

	One-Second (1.0) Response Time	*Ten-Second (10.0) Response Time*
Modem	2 KB	34 KB
ISDN	8 KB	150 KB
T1	100 KB	2 MB

Figure 2.3   File Size and Response Times Based on Internet Connection (Nielsen 2000, 28)

Links

Links are the cornerstone of the web and provide the ability to connect to additional documents for more information. Several guidelines for properly displaying links will ensure visitors enjoy their user experience.

- Place the link on the most important word or phrase as it relates in context to the link's destination so that visitors will have no question about where the link will take them. Avoid links that include an entire sentence.
- Avoid wrapping links from one line to the next because visitors will view them as two separate links although they link to the same destination.
- Use standard link colors, if possible, such as blue and purple.
- Using graphics as links fails to provide users with a visual cue that they have previously visited the web page. Include a text link to the same destination page that will turn a different color once visited.
- Links, in most cases, should not open up a new browser because this limits the users' ability to continue their surfing by pressing the back button.

Writing for the Web

Differences in online and offline reading tendencies necessitate that documents destined for the Web be prepared differently than those intended for print publication. Reading from computer screens is 25 percent slower than reading from paper (Nielsen 2000). As visitors search through the site looking for information, it is much easier to skim through chunks of information rather than verbose text-laden pages. Designers can accommodate this slower pace by converting text into brief paragraphs and bulleted lists. Other techniques include using more nouns and verbs than adverbs and adjectives and flushing text to the left instead of centering it. Designers may also want to include printer-friendly pages so that visitors may print materials for offline reading. Printer-friendly pages are typically prepared in a standard font and are free of images.

Many time designers are asked to post brochures and newsletters on the web site that have been previously prepared for print publication. Creating bibliographies, user guides, and newsletters takes a great deal of staff time, so it is important to be able to recycle content on the web site; however, the content must be edited so that it is written from a web user's perspective. For example, many print publications include invitations for the reader to visit the web site. This would be redundant should the invitation appear on the web site.

Web Site Requirements

Certain elements should maintain their consistency as visitors move from one page to the next within a web site. Users also expect to see consistency throughout each page, such as access to the main navigation bar, web page titles, footers, authoring agent, copyright statement, date, and last revision date. It is also important that functionality remain consistent throughout the site. For example, including forms that may be submitted electronically would be incongruent if other forms must be printed and faxed. Users expect a certain amount of uniformity throughout the web site.

Forms. The inclusion of forms on a library web site is one of the easiest ways to add interactivity to the site by providing a way for visitors to interact with the library and its staff. Forms can be used for a variety of purposes, such as library card applications, interlibrary loans requests, and room reservations. Forms can be submitted electronically or displayed for online completion and printing. If the form is not for electronic submission, then visitors expect to be able to fill the form out online for printing and subsequent faxing or mailing. Users will not take kindly to printing and handwriting forms available online, nor should the user be expected to complete the form using a typewriter. The library should make sure that if electronic submission is not an option, the user can complete the form online.

There are several ways to ensure that forms created for electronic submission enhance the user's visit. Fields must allow users adequate space for the amount of text expected. Additionally, any required fields should be designated with an asterisk; however, if the form is filled out incorrectly or the user has not entered information into a required field, the web site should let them know which fields were not filled out properly. Once the user submits the incomplete form, the resulting page should highlight the fields that are incomplete yet maintain the information the user has already entered. The user should not have to retype the information already input.

If the form is expected to generate a lot of submissions, then a separate e-mail account should be set up specifically for this purpose. Additionally, by customizing the subject line of the e-mail, the results of more than one form can be easily managed within the same e-mail account. The following HTML tag inserted within the form designates the subject line of the e-mails generated:

<input name="subject" type="hidden" value="enter subject line here">.

Forms that visitors complete to enter a program, such as summer reading, would be more appropriately sent to a database instead of an e-mail account.

This method will best help sort statistics, especially if demographic information is collected (age, grade level, etc.).

Logo. The library logo should appear on all web pages within the site and is most appropriately placed on the top or the top left corner of the page. Although the logo should be prominent, it should not overpower the overall design of the page nor be so large that it pushes the content further down on the screen. The logo should serve as a link to the home page from any page in the site.

FAQs. Frequently asked questions (FAQs) should be compiled from the questions asked by the public regarding the use of the web site. Library web sites that have more than one FAQs site can place them in the section titled About This Site. Various FAQs, such as those written to address questions about accessing electronic books or the library catalog, can be listed there. Some of the questions include how to renew materials online or access research databases.

Feedback. Webmasters should not miss the opportunity to receive feedback from their visitors in the form of e-mail. Visitors should be able to easily e-mail the webmaster from any page on the site or through a Contact Us button displayed on the main navigation bar. Gathering comments from visitors will assist in minor adjustments and site redesigns.

Error Pages. Hypertext Transfer Protocol (HTTP) errors users are most likely to encounter are 404 Not Found (the URL is not on the server), 403 Forbidden (the server's configuration forbids it from providing the URL), 401 Unauthorized (the requested page requires authentication), and 500 Internal Server Error (something on the server has gone wrong) (Dowling 2003). Error messages should include an explanation of why the user's transaction failed and include a clear exit point. Error messages originating from the library catalog should be customized to include the same information as web site error pages. Test vendor products for error page customization, too. Although licensed databases are produced by third-party vendors, an unsuccessful search for information reflects poorly on the library.

Contact Information. Include contact information such as telephone number and address on the home page. Each web page within the site should link to a Contact Us button that will list all library departments, branches, and services. Including links to map services such as MapQuest so that users can quickly find directions is also helpful.

Testing Techniques

Usability testing is an iterative process that includes gathering data and information about the web site and using this feedback to improve the site. Testing may be applied to certain parts of the site or the entire site. Once results of the test are considered and applied to the prototype, test again to see if the changes were successful. Usability testing can (1) diagnose problems, (2) compare alternatives, and (3) verify that you have met usability goals (National Cancer Institute). Usability testing is important for the following reasons (Pace 2003):

Testing saves the user time and saves the organization time and money.

Testing counters the whim of designers.

Testing is good public relations for the organization offering online services.

Testing settles disagreements among design team members, whether stated or unstated.

There are several ways that web managers can test their site for usability. One of the easiest and most inexpensive ways to do this is to choose a few tasks that volunteers can perform on the web site. Ask them to think aloud and record all of the steps it takes them to complete each task. Questions should assess whether visitors were able to easily complete a task, perform some function, or find information. Some examples of tasks to use follow:

Find an article about Colin Powell.

Renew your library materials.

Apply for a library card.

Is the library open on a Sunday?

Does the library own the March 1988 issue of The New Yorker?

Because of the shifting nature of the Internet, user testing must become part of site maintenance.

For more information

Campbell, Nicole, ed. 2001. *Usability assessment of library-related web sites: Methods and case studies.* Chicago: LITA.

Computers in Libraries. 2003. Vol. 23, no. 1 (January).

This issue deals with usability including articles such as "The Mom-and-Pop-Shop Approach to Usability Studies," "A Tale of Two Needs: Usability Testing and Library Orientation," "Getting Two for the Price of One: Accessibility and Usability," and "Earning the Stamp of Approval: How to Achieve Optimal Usability."

Norlin, Elaina, and CM! Winters. *Usability testing for library web sites.* Chicago: ALA, 2001.

Pace, Andrew K. 2002. Optimizing library web services: A usability approach. *Library Technology Reports* 38, no. 2 (March/April).

THREE

Internet Marketing: Promoting the Library

A successful library web site is viewed not only as a delivery mechanism for online services, but also as a tool to promote *all* library services. The library web site carries enterprise-wide implications for promoting awareness of all library services, including information about the library as an organization and community resource. Libraries will continue to carry out more of their business online and should realize that their web site is a marketing tool, not just a means of delivering services and information. This chapter focuses on the use of the web site to further promote library collections and services rather than the external promotion of the web site to its users.

Libraries will find that although their users come to the web site to use the library catalog and research databases, many users come to learn about events, services, employment, volunteer opportunities, foundations, and friends' groups. Creating "sticky content" (that is, intriguing information above and beyond checking books out) keeps visitors lingering for longer periods of time. Additionally, online newsletters can be used to promote various parts of the web site as well as offline library events and services.

BRANDING AND THE LIBRARY IMAGE

Throughout its pages, a web site must display consistency with the use of its logo, writing style, and design. In fact, using a similar style within print and online publications not only reduces the duplication of efforts involved in creating print graphics and online publications, but it also provides patrons with a consistent look and feel that can be achieved with a recognizable logo, a familiar color scheme, and design. Ideally, a library's print publications and web site should interact with one another. Print newsletters, brochures, and bookmarks should invite people to the web site so they may interact in some way such as submitting a book review or poem or searching the catalog or a research database.

Taglines

What do the following phrases have in common?

"All the news that's fit to print."

"It takes a licking and keeps on ticking."

"M'm! M'm! Good!"

These taglines are ingrained in Americans' minds and associated with a brand name. Taglines are phrases or short sentences that sum up what you do in a few words. Examples of taglines that libraries can use follow:

Your Library on the Internet

Expand Your Internet Search

Your Library, Something for Everyone

Access Your Library from Home

Other engaging taglines come from the Milwaukee (Wis.) Public Library *(Every Person's Gateway)*, Atlanta-Fulton (Ga.) Public Library System *(The People's University)*, Detroit (Mich.) Public Library *(Your Information Destination)*, and Omaha (Neb.) Public Library *(Everything You Want to Know. And More)*. Placement of taglines should be close to the logo and included in the title tag of the home page. Using the same phrase on print materials that advertise the web site should reinforce the message the library is trying to convey.

ABOUT THE LIBRARY

Visitors come to the library's web site for a variety of reasons ranging from finding employment and volunteer opportunities, learning about the community, and locating board of trustee information to accessing research materials. Many visitors come to the library's web site to learn more about the library's services, both online and offline. The web site provides an opportunity to market those services that may not be visible to users in the physical library because they occur behind-the-scenes. These include interlibrary loan, electronic reserves, and services for special populations such as distance education students or the homebound. Figure 1.4 in chapter 1 provides an inventory checklist noting content that libraries typically include on their web sites, and it can be used to determine what content should be placed in this section. This checklist is also available on this book's companion web site at http://www.webliography.org.

Services

One of the most difficult challenges that libraries face is the hunt for meaningful words and phrases describing library services in terms users can understand. A web site that is intuitive for users will seamlessly incorporate library services and collections into its pages. Users should not be required to decode library terminology nor guess where a link may take them. Libraries must reengineer their thinking about how they present their services to the public. How can libraries best present their services in a manner in which patrons will understand? It is impossible to promote something when you cannot accurately describe it to a potential audience.

Libraries currently use the following terms to describe their services: *reference services, user services, adult services,* and *borrower services.* Perhaps the single term *services* would suffice. It is this type of situation where marketing, usability, and information architecture meet. By focusing priority on user-centered design the problem comes close to a solution. Determine what users come to the site for, predict what they may be looking for, and study site statistics. These tactics are used to best determine how to present and market library services on the web site.

Perhaps in the earlier days of the Internet, visitors to the library web site may have had the following thought: "What can I do online?" However, now visitors expect to find online services. Some libraries have chosen to highlight their online services with terms like *electronic resources, e-library, virtual library services,* and *online resources.* However important it is to highlight interactive services, it is just as critical that they are also found in context where visitors would generally look for them within the web site. For example, on the library's Good Books page, a link to subscription products like NoveList or What Do I Read Next? would be appropriate (as well as being listed on the online database page). The more content and services that continue to come online, the more difficult it will be to maintain a portion of the web site strictly for online services, or an e-branch, because most visitors will assume it is all online.

Events and Programming

Offering events and programs takes a considerable amount of staff time and effort. Additionally, many community groups use the library as a meeting place. Libraries offering events such as story time, tax preparation services, homework help centers, book discussion groups, film series, and other regular events have a continual stream of content to offer their visitors. This information provides the library site with regularly changing content to keep its site looking fresh but presents a challenge on how to manage it.

Libraries should reserve a spot on the home page specifically for displaying upcoming events and any graphics associated with them. Although community use of library rooms may occur, library-sponsored events should take precedence, and, ideally, a listing of all events should be made available. Events with large venues should be posted on the home page, whereas events with smaller attendance, such as book discussion groups, can be highlighted in context, on pages that readers would most likely visit (i.e., the Good Books page). Additionally, events the library offers can often support companion content that works well together. For example, Banned Books Week, a highly celebrated event, can be paired with a bibliography of challenged materials linked into the catalog.

Displaying home page graphics can be done so that the web page changes upon refreshing one's browser, or each time a visitor accesses the page. It is important, however, that if you chose to rotate graphics, information about the event is static and that only the graphic changes. That way the user does not have to continually refresh the browser to find information on the event. So, it is important that more than one graphic be created and used in the rotation. Presenters, artists, and authors will normally provide promotional photographs or images depicting their event.

Because of the structural nature of the type of information associated with events and programs (time, date, program, location), it is appropriate to create a database. In fact, in a multibranch library system that offers a lot of programming, a database-driven web page would be most appropriate. Some issues to consider follow:

Staff involvement: involve staff who will be entering the data into the design process *before* building the system.

Editorial guidelines: create guidelines for data entry so that results posted to a web page mirror guidelines imposed on the rest of the site.

Print publications: create a process so that once programs are published to print format, they are also input into the events database.

Adaptable system: the system must be built for change (i.e., if a new type of event is added, a new category can be created, or date ranges for exhibits can be added in addition to dates for one-day events).

Foundations, Fund-Raising, and Friends

Libraries will find that publishing information regarding the library foundation, fund-raising efforts, and the friends of the library groups offers additional opportunities not only to promote their causes and increase membership and donations, but also to generate income online. Some friends' groups are selling discarded materials and donations on eBay or other online auction houses. Foundations are soliciting donations through their web sites (*see* figure 3.1), and some libraries have partnered with Amazon.com to sell books so they may receive a percentage of the sale. Libraries are just beginning to test the water, and using the Internet as a channel for philanthropic and entrepreneurial efforts is an area that has yet to evolve.

Some patrons would prefer to purchase a book depending upon its availability at the library, and some libraries can partner with bookstores so that they receive a percentage of the sale (*see* figure 3.2). Libraries should explore the

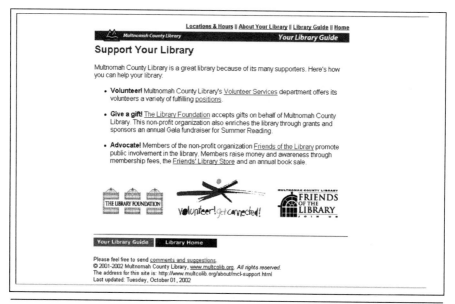

Figure 3.1 Support Your Library, Multnomah County (Ore.) Library. The Multnomah County Library posts a page on how visitors can help the library (http://www.multcolib.org/about/mcl-support.html).

Figure 3.2 Public Library of Charlotte and Mecklenburg County (N.C.) Reader's Club. Visitors are offered the opportunity to purchase materials through Amazon.com, which will donate a portion of the sale to the library (http://www.readersclub.org/support.asp).

pros and cons of offering a link to online bookstores, including (1) the link sends patrons away from the catalog, (2) the choice of an online-only or chain bookstore could show lack of support for local bookstores, and (3) becoming an affiliate of the bookstore may place the library in the role of promoting or endorsing one bookstore over another.

CREATING STICKY CONTENT

As mentioned, nothing keeps visitors lingering on web sites more than intriguing and attention-grabbing content, known as sticky content. This can range from a variety of topics; however, the best content is usually local. Local, library-related, and relevant content will engage your visitors and keep them coming back for more.

Content Ideas, Some Free

Ideas for content can come from virtually anywhere. First, look internally for content (special collections, supplementary information for successful programs and events, materials to accompany a library class). Look outside of the library to government and nonprofit agencies, local historians, and other libraries. Put the word out and ask others to be your eyes and ears for suitable content. Libraries can even use their web site to request submissions from the community. If libraries embark on a digitization project, they can often negotiate to lease material until it has been digitized and return it to the owner.

This book will provide you with more ideas within each chapter, such as the ways libraries can add value to information through obituary indexes and referral services. (*See* chapter 4.) The following are other ideas for sticky content for your library web site.

Submissions from the Community

Local photos, old postcards, recipes

Local history of ethnic groups in the community

Oral histories from the community's elderly population

Citizen's guide to local government

Book reviews

Content for School-Aged Kids

Partner with teachers to generate ongoing content such as student essays, science projects, poetry, and book reviews.

General Interest

Public domain materials

U.S. government information that can be repackaged

Free content from vendors who may offer high-interest content for a limited time

Images and Multimedia Files

Images can be used for a variety of reasons; most important, images—including photographs, illustrations, and clip art—aid in web site navigation. The same color and text used on images for navigating the web site should also be used in the library catalog. Additionally, images can be created to depict events for promotional purposes. Because many events may occur annually, it is wise to archive images so they may be used again. It is also important to note that many of the events promoted on the web site will quite possibly be promoted in print publications. Images prepared for print publication can be scaled down to a suitable file size for display on the Web; however, web graphics display poorly in print. Formatting graphics for print materials and web display not only provides readers and visitors with a consistent message, but it also saves time and money.

In addition to creating custom graphics, libraries can also purchase images from companies that offer online libraries of images that can be used for print and online use. The service is similar to companies that offer stock photography. Prices for images depend on usage, whether the use is for print or online. For example, you may purchase images of seniors or children for use on the web site. The images can be purchased and downloaded from the vendor or sent on a CD-ROM.

Multimedia files include sound, graphics, video images, animations, and text. Because of their heavy file sizes, they should be used sparingly throughout the web site where they are relevant to content. Some examples of content that justify the inclusion of multimedia include offering audio files that support the publication of an oral history project, including videos to enhance an interactive tutorial, or adding audio to demonstrate music. As described in chapter 8, web designers should consider providing secondary access to the content for accessibility and usability concerns. For example, offering transcripts in text alongside audio files allows screen readers to access this information or users to read the transcripts before investing the time necessary to access the audio file.

Newsletters

Libraries develop newsletters to create awareness and promote collections and services. Print newsletters are normally sent to registered patrons and distributed to local organizations, branch libraries, or satellite campuses. An electronic newsletter offers advantages to print including a tremendous savings on the costs of publishing, timeliness, and distribution. Electronic newsletters reach their audience immediately, and links throughout the newsletter will drive users through your web site as they click through to points of interest. Users manage their own subscriptions by subscribing and unsubscribing through the web site. Last, not only does the library provide a new way to maintain communication with its current customer base, but the library also has an effective way to communicate with remote audiences.

The print and online versions of the library newsletter can actually complement each other. The print newsletter can drive patrons to your web site by offering them more content. For example, a few sentences describing a new research database purchase in the print newsletter can conclude with an invitation to visit the web site. The online version includes the same description with a link to the page where the database is accessible.

Every issue should include the name of the newsletter, date or issue number, instructions on how to unsubscribe, a link to the library's privacy statement, library contact information, and where archives can be found, if applicable.

Content and editorial concerns. Library newsletters include a host of topics such as library news (new automation systems, new hours, director's message, foundation and donations); library research material (databases, new web site content, library collections); and library events (programs, instruction). Determining the content of the online newsletter should involve a review of library goals and objectives as well as the newsletter's intended audience.

Library goals and objectives. Review library planning documents. What objectives will publishing the newsletter help achieve? Will the newsletter aid in promotion of online collections and services or physical collections and events? Determine how the newsletter can aid in achieving established goals and objectives defined in the library's planning documents. The needs of the library community, coupled with existing library goals, should drive content. For example, the library has determined that a primary goal is to increase student usage of research databases. One objective of that goal reads, "By 2005, faculty members will routinely include use of research databases in their assignments, and online database usage will increase by 30 percent." Because awareness of databases precedes use, the library may determine that an online newsletter written for faculty highlighting research databases may be an appropriate use of staff time and efforts.

Authoring the newsletter. Public relations specialists typically author library newsletters; however, frontline library staff should be involved in developing its content. Brandt discusses "customer service redundancies" when he describes how easy it is for libraries to create content for their newsletters: "The information is redundant, in the sense that it comes straight out of some other source: acquisitions list, new product descriptions, newsletters. But it is repackaged for each group based on their needs and desires" (Brandt 2001, 62).

Frequency. Libraries must determine if the newsletter should be published weekly, biweekly, monthly, or quarterly. The decision should be based on availability of content and staff resources to keep the frequency consistent.

Length. Keep the length of the newsletter to a minimum and follow the basic usability principles discussed in chapter 2. Some newsletters are structured so that the e-mail includes an abridged version with a link to the full newsletter archived on the web site.

File formats. File formats should facilitate access. Libraries may be tempted to create a newsletter in PDF (Adobe's portable document format) because of its visual appeal; however, sending PDF files via e-mail brings up a rash of accessibility issues: (1) file size can be prohibitive, (2) the user must have Adobe Acrobat, and (3) PDF files may provide an additional impediment to users with low or no vision. A text-based e-mail is preferable to all other formats because it requires only that the recipient have an e-mail account. Libraries may find that creating their newsletters in a plain e-mail text with a link to the full version located on the web site works well. (*See* figure 3.3.)

Software. Software exists that will automate the management of e-mail lists. Prices are quoted based upon single or multiple lists of contacts and the number of subscribers. E-mail list management software should be able to (1) automate subscription handling, (2) manage undeliverable e-mails, and (3) return reports that count the number of current subscribers, new subscribers, unsubscribers, and the elapsed time for sending out the e-mails.

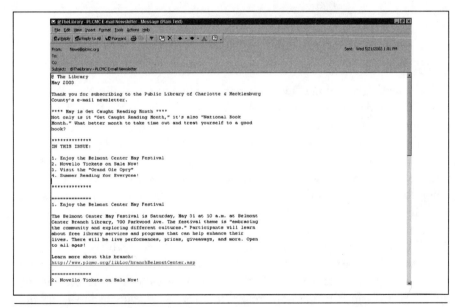

Figure 3.3 E-mail Newsletter, Public Library of Charlotte and Mecklenburg County (N.C.). The Public Library of Charlotte and Mecklenburg County authors their newsletter in text, with links to further information.

FOUR

Digital Reference Collections and Services

The introduction of new technology has forced librarianship to continually adapt its outlook on delivering services and maintaining collections. Enter the telephone, facsimile machine, telecommunications device for the deaf (TDD), optical scanners, electronic mail, FTP, electronic bulletin boards, and the World Wide Web, and one can see why it is true that librarianship has continued to expand, extend, and reinvent itself throughout history. More than any other changes, new technology has offered librarianship both challenges and opportunities in providing reference services using a medium very much accepted and enjoyed by the general public.

The Web has probably affected reference services more than it has any other facet of librarianship. Its collections, through major digitization efforts and third-party vendors, are now available with round-the-clock access through the library web site. Furthermore, many libraries now provide twenty-four-hour customer access to librarians able to answer questions and assist users via electronic chat. For visitors accustomed to web surfing, libraries can now be visited with a minimum of effort, a point and click away.

Although digital reference services evoke a new set of rules, standards for traditional reference service may be applied when developing library services. Librarians must remember that it is not the service but the mode of delivery that is new. The software allows both patrons and information to connect with one another by means of an intermediary, the librarian. *Guidelines for Information Services* created by ALA's Reference and User Services Association (RUSA) provides a baseline for staff to follow when providing information services. The guidelines state that libraries should provide the information sought by the user; develop information, reference, and directional services; offer finding aids to help users identify relevant items in the collection; provide instruction in the effective use of its resources; provide access to the services and resources of local organizations; add value to information if not useful as presented in its current form; and refer either the user or the question to another agency, expert, or other library.

Librarians can bring reference services online by providing local digitized content, e-mail and chat reference service, and content such as frequently asked questions and knowledge bases, instruction and training, collections of web site links, and value-added content such as obituary indexes and referral services. Librarians add value to information when they organize, annotate, and create retrieval mechanisms.

DIGITAL COLLECTIONS

Libraries worldwide are digitizing materials and offering full-text documents or images to patrons via their web sites. Digital collections usually consist of local content and provide unlimited access to materials that are not readily accessible. These projects create digital copies and aid in the preservation of the original material by saving wear and tear inherent with public use.

Libraries can begin by identifying collections of materials to digitize, finding copyright owners, or declaring the materials within the public domain. Depending on the content of the materials (text, graphics, or both) and their quality, standards should be developed by which to capture their representation by scanning, photographing, or other means. Finally, libraries must identify the most effective way to index or catalog the materials in order to create a retrieval system. Budgetary concerns include staff, computers and other equipment, electronic publishing costs, and web programming.

One of the most well known and largest digitization collections is *American Memory* (http://lcweb2.loc.gov/ammem), sponsored by the Library of Congress. This collection has more than 7 million digital items from more than 100 historical collections in formats such as photographs, manuscripts, rare books, maps, recorded sound, and moving pictures. Web researchers will also benefit from the New York Public Library's digital image collection (http://digital.nypl.org), a total of 600,000 images including artwork, maps, photographs, prints, manuscripts, illustrated books, and printed ephemera. Collections are diverse and intrinsically valuable, providing researchers with access to myriad topics that were previously difficult to access or unknown.

Libraries can find collections worthy of digitizing by taking inventory of their own special collections or by contacting local organizations that may have collections but not the means to digitize them. Libraries can build digital collections of local resources through partnerships with local organizations, museums, and government agencies. Academic libraries can also find digitization projects from other university departments, private collections of noted professors, or famous alumni. For example, a donation from author Stephen King makes up the collections of the Stephen Edward King papers at the University of Maine's Fogler Library.

For more information

ARL Digital Initiatives Database
http://www.arl.org/did

> This database describes digital initiatives in or involving libraries sponsored by the University of Illinois at Chicago and ARL.

Digital Library Federation
http://www.diglib.org

> A consortium of libraries providing leadership in the creation of digital collections and publisher of *D-Lib Magazine.*

IFLA—Digital Libraries Resources and Projects
http://www.ifla.org/II/diglib.htm

> Publishes and organizes information relating to digital libraries. Sponsor of DIGLIB mailing list.

E-MAIL AND CHAT REFERENCE SERVICE

E-mail was introduced into reference services as early as the mid-1980s, and since that time, the field of virtual reference has continued to grow, as evidenced by the increasing amount of professional literature as well as conferences dedicated solely to this topic. Companies have created software specifically for real-time reference, in many cases developed using e-commerce models. Libraries have been involved in developing and defining the field and working on many issues surrounding virtual reference, such as creating standards, collaborating and staffing, addressing budget concerns, marketing the service, training, and evaluating.

Chat reference is synonymous with the following phrases used to describe "real-time human help delivered through the Internet" (Meola and Stormont 2002, 13): "live reference," "real-time reference," "virtual reference," and "synchronous reference." For as many terms used in the library field, there are just as many terms used to describe the same service to the public through the library's web site: Ask Me, Ask a Librarian, Answers Unlimited, Chat with a Librarian, Librarians Online. Naming the service aids in marketing the service within the print world; however, when presented in the context of the web site, when users have already arrived at the web site, a link to "help" may be what drives visitors to use the service. Most recently, libraries have begun placing all of the ways that they offer reference services—by telephone, e-mail, live chat, visits, and by appointment—on their web sites (as illustrated in figure 4.1).

Reference Interview through Forms and Text Boxes

Although the reference interview has been discussed and written about extensively, e-mail reference attempts to gather as much information from the patron within a form. At minimum, the following fields appear in e-mail reference

Figure 4.1   Ask! a Librarian, Yale University Library (Conn.). The Yale University Library publishes a variety of ways its customers may ask questions (http://www.library.yale.edu/reference/asklive/index.html).

forms: name, e-mail address, library card number, deadline, question, sources already consulted, and grade level. The goal of the form is to elicit certain responses from the patron to minimize the number of electronic exchanges involved in an online reference question. This is, of course, more noticeable within an e-mail transaction rather than live chat because the customer and the librarian can chat back and forth until the query is refined. A question submitted through e-mail, on the other hand, may require several transactions spanning several days. Therein shows the shortcomings of e-mail reference, because in many cases, the transaction falls off when the patron does not respond or takes too long to respond to follow-up questions or types his or her e-mail address incorrectly into the form.

Although chat reference forms are normally not so explicit and may contain a simple text box, the reference interview begins with several exchanges between library and patron over the course of a few minutes. The immediacy of chat reference allows easier flow of communication so that the reference interview can be carried out without the difficulties of e-mail reference.

Point of Need

Patrons may need assistance at any point of their visit to the library web site, at any hour, and within any system, including the library catalog or any one of the library's third-party research databases. Libraries must find a way to incorporate their online reference service into vendor's screens of research databases so that users can contact their own librarians versus sending an e-mail to the vendor's information technology department. Patrons should be presented, at any time and within any screen, with a help button that connects them with live help. Because the library catalog is web-based and customizable, graphics and links can normally be inserted into the catalog with minimal efforts; however, vendors of third-party databases should allow libraries the ability to place a link to online help within their screens.

Standards

In most cases, if any policies or guidelines are made available to the public, they tend to address issues of patron privacy and service restrictions but fail to address guidelines and standards that a librarian would consult, such as those approved by the American Library Association for other services. The IFLA Digital Reference Standards Project identified the following groups involved in creating digital reference guidelines and standards (IFLA 2002):

Machine-Assisted Reference Section (MARS)
http://www.ala.org/Content/NavigationMenu/RUSA/Our_Association2/
RUSA_Sections/MARS/MARS.htm

MARS, a part of the Reference and User Services Association of ALA, focuses on digital reference services, document delivery, and networked information resources. MARS has created a Virtual Reference Discussion Group and a Digital Reference Guidelines Ad Hoc Committee, whose focus is on creating standards for digital reference services.

The National Information Standards Organization (NISO)
http://www.niso.org/committees/committee_az.html

NISO's creation of standards for digital reference services focuses on the processing and routing of questions and responses, the development of data element sets to identify and describe key components of questions and answers, and the institutions and staff who answer the questions.

Virtual Reference Desk (VRD) Project
http://www.vrd.org

VRD Project, sponsored by the U.S. Department of Education, is dedicated to the advancement of digital reference and the successful creation and operation of human-mediated, Internet-based information services. VRD coordinates a network of ASKa services so that each service serves the other by answering overflow questions outside of the subject scope. VRD holds an annual conference and sponsors DIG-REF, an electronic discussion list that explores digital reference service. VRD also publishes *Facets of Quality for Digital Reference Services* (http://www.vrd.org/training/facets.html), which outlines important characteristics and features for building digital reference services.

Collaboration

Because of the staff intensiveness of providing live reference services, as well as finding funding for software costs, many libraries have joined together to provide this service to their patrons. "Collaborative reference is two or more libraries deciding to work together and share resources (staff, hardware, software) to offer reference services to users at participating institutions" (Meola and Stormont 2002, 12). Relationships among libraries include state cooperatives, sister libraries from across the world located in different time zones, and libraries banding together with a common goal.

Some examples of collaboration follow:

KnowItNow24x7
> http://www.knowitnow24x7.net
>
> Serves Cuyahoga County, Ohio, and the communities of the CLEVNET Libraries

My Web Librarian
> http://www.myweblibrarian.com
>
> A merger of the Alliance Library System (Ready for Reference) and North Suburban Library System (Answers Unlimited) of Illinois

Q and A Café
> http://www.QandAcafe.com
>
> Libraries in the greater San Francisco, Monterey Bay, and North Bay for the state of California with the Metropolitan Cooperative Library System in southern California

Q and A NJ
> http://www.qandanj.org
>
> A 24/7 service from member libraries of the New Jersey Library Network

For more information

Bernie Sloan's Digital Reference Pages
> http://alexia.lis.uiuc.edu/~b-sloan/bernie.htm

Going Live: Starting and Running a Virtual Reference Service by Steve Coffman (Chicago: ALA, 2003)

LiveRef(sm): A Registry of Real-Time Digital Reference Services
> http://www.public.iastate.edu/~CYBERSTACKS/LiveRef.htm

FREQUENTLY ASKED REFERENCE QUESTIONS (FARQS)

Libraries are fairly consistent in saving information for a later date in hopes that it will help answer the same question in the future so as not to replicate research. Frequently Asked Reference Questions (FARQs) have also been used as very effective training tools for new staff. Librarians have been capturing this information in a vertical file or Rolodex for years. The Web offers the opportunity to make this information available to our patrons even before they ask the question. Libraries are turning print files and index cards into web pages. Libraries should offer information such as date last verified and source of the information.

Examples

Fugitive Facts Hennepin County (Minn.) Library
 http://www.hclib.org/pub/search/fff_public.cfm

Internet Public Library's Frequently Asked Reference Questions
 http://www.ipl.org/div/farq/

KNOWLEDGE BASES

Recently the term *knowledge base* has been used within librarianship to describe the accumulated information as a result of answered questions. Knowledge bases are different from databases in that (1) they not only store data, but also facilitate modification, revision, and other forms of internal manipulation of the knowledge; (2) they are also able to handle knowledge that is incomplete, inconsistent, and uncertain; and (3) they may use imperative as well as declarative forms of knowledge (*Dictionary of Computing* 1996). Knowledge bases, in virtual reference circles, are accumulated questions and answers that have been edited, placed in a database, and made searchable to the public (as illustrated in figure 4.2). Implications for libraries include privacy and patron confidentiality. Although patron information is stripped from the knowledge database, there are other privacy concerns dealing with the content of the questions. For instance, if the question deals with the area of intellectual property (patents, trademarks), patrons may be reluctant to ask the question or may have to actively craft the question so as not to reveal trade secrets or potential product ideas. Also, questions about people, outside of a genealogy request, may involve others' personal names. Patrons can opt out of including their question in the knowledge base; however, many may not understand the implications involved. Libraries should beware of the impact this may have on their patron's willingness to ask his or her question on the Web.

Example

Virtual Information Desk Keystone Library (Pa.) Network
 http://libweb.mansfield.edu/vid/vid-kb.asp

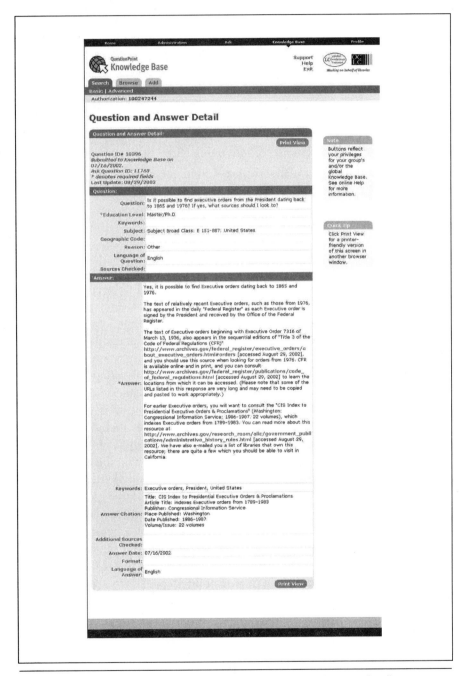

Figure 4.2 QuestionPoint Knowledge Base (OCLC) Question and Answer Detail

WEB-BASED INSTRUCTION

The Web offers libraries a unique opportunity to extend the teaching experience to their visitors through a variety of methods covering an assortment of topics such as library orientation and tours, guides to the collection, *webquests* (discussed further below), and tutorials. Web-based instruction also offers libraries the opportunity to interact with distance education students like never before. Some common topics for tutorials include searching the library catalog, learning information literacy skills, finding periodicals and journal articles, and software-specific searching in online databases (*see* figure 4.3). Once created, web-based curricula must be continually updated because updates to the catalog and changes to the online database subscriptions and functionality may impact content of the instruction.

In addition to applying basic web design principles to its development, ACRL's Communication Committee has developed the following *Tips for Developing Effective Web-Based Library Instruction* (ACRL 2003):

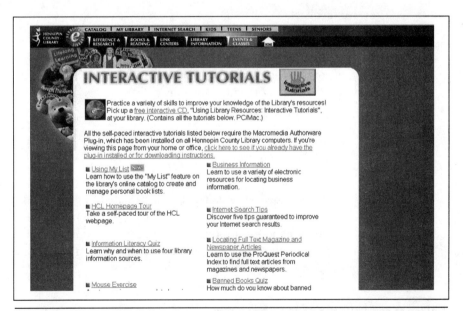

Figure 4.3 Interactive Tutorials, Hennepin County (Minn.) Library. Interactive Tutorials, available at the Hennepin County Library, include a tour of their web page, an information literacy quiz, and a tutorial on locating full-text magazine and newspaper articles. These self-paced tutorials require the Macromedia Authorware plug-in to view (http://www.hclib.org/pub/training).

1. Outline the objectives and outcomes clearly to establish purpose and realistic expectations.
2. Provide a clearly defined structure that:
   a. reflects the objectives of the tutorial and
   b. allows for both linear and nonlinear learning, so students can review sections and/or select the pathways that best meet their needs
3. Include interactive exercises (active learning) such as with simulations, manipulation of objects, interactive quizzes, or the direct application of principles. These will encourage problem solving by students and allow them to:
   a. practice/respond to what is taught
   b. self-assess their learning
   c. engage in "deep learning" (understanding the meaning) rather than "surface learning" (memorization and regurgitation)
   d. receive feedback
4. Give attention to the concepts behind the mechanics so that information skills are applicable to other search interfaces.
5. Incorporate contemporary language and topics, be as succinct as possible, and don't be afraid to entertain. This will:
   a. establish relevance to students' lives
   b. not overwhelm them with verbiage and
   c. help to keep their interest
6. Provide a way to contact a librarian.
7. When the tutorial is used, try to make it course-related by encouraging faculty to link web-based instruction to a course assignment. This will provide additional hands-on experiences using information resources in various formats within the context of an actual assignment, further reinforcing the tutorial's teachings and relevance.

Guides to the Collection and Virtual Tours

Guides to the collection and virtual tours weave text and graphics together to inform users about the contents of collections and their physical locations. They include bibliographic materials within special collections, services, and visual representations of their physical space. The intent of their creation is to provide patrons with information to acclimate them to the collection prior to visiting the library.

Examples

Guides to the Library, Boston Public Library
http://www.bpl.org/guides/index.htm

> Guides to the Library, a choice on the main navigation bar, offers visitors a variety of content, including library history, descriptions of the library's art and architecture, and maps of library locations and building floor plans.

Panoramic Views of the Tempe (Ariz.) Public Library
http://www.tempe.gov/library/360/

> These web pages display 360-degree views of various locations within the library. When the mouse is placed over the photo, users can either click and drag for more viewer control or press A or + to zoom in and Z or - to zoom out.

Public Library of Charlotte and Mecklenburg County (N.C.)
http://www.plcmc.org/multimedia/default.htm

> These multimedia tours include the history of the library, an overview of major services, architectural tours of PLCMC facilities, and the Brarydog research portal. PLCMC uses Flash to produce some of their guides.

Virtual Tours, Las Vegas–Clark County Library District
http://www.lvccld.org/ref_info/virtual_tours/index.htm

> The library provides virtual tours of community resources. Staff document the visit with photographs and information about the services these local agencies provide.

Pathfinders and Research Guides

Librarians author pathfinders and research guides as part of what they do, so bringing them online does not require too much work because the documents are already created. What makes these guides so attractive is that librarians are able to point researchers to all relevant materials regardless of location on the web site. For instance, links can be made to items in the catalog, online databases, e-books, web sites, library programs, and other pages within the library web site. Pathfinders and research guides are also easily updated and maintained, accessible any time of the day, and, if designed properly, can be printed from the web site for class visits and distribution.

Although the initial amount of staff time needed to create pathfinders is often exorbitant, when finished, pathfinders save staff time and add a heightened awareness of available resources. Traditional research guides, much more comprehensive than pathfinders, include categories like encyclopedias, dictionaries, guides and handbooks, directories, magazines, organizations, bibliographies, and indexes.

Five pointers for publishing pathfinders and research guides follow:

1. Open a new browser when pointing to an external link so that users can refer back to it.
2. Use a library card image to indicate that certain resources may only be accessed with a library card number.
3. Create a navigation bar at the top of the document to assist your users in surfing within the document.
4. Keep the pathfinder to a length of no more than two pages; however, because research guides are much more comprehensive, the librarian should determine its length based on necessity.
5. Create printer-friendly or PDF formats of the guide.

Webquests

A relatively new type of instruction, the webquest, an inquiry-oriented activity that challenges students to not just find, but analyze, synthesize, and evaluate web-based information, was developed at San Diego State University in early 1995 by Bernie Dodge. The webquest is oriented toward schools and academia because of its evaluative component and collaborative nature. However, webquests may be adapted to be of use in public libraries. Webquests differ from traditional research assignments in their organizational structure and are customarily divided into sections: introduction, task, resources, process, evaluation, and conclusion (Braun 2001). Webquests are not widely used in public libraries, and opportunities for development in this area exist, especially in partnership with school libraries. Webquests involve the use of a rubric, a tool for measuring the student's success.

Example

Four NETS for Better Searching
   http://webquest.sdsu.edu/searching/fournets.htm

   Teaches search engine skills by narrowing the query, searching with exact phrases, trimming back the URL for more information, and finding similar pages

Tutorials

Tutorials aim to teach a skill by taking sequential steps to achieve an objective. Students should be made aware of what they will learn, how long it will take to complete the tutorial, and any plug-ins necessary to view it. Tutorials may also offer a way to evaluate what was learned.

Examples

Pennsylvania State University
http://www.libraries.psu.edu/instruction/tutorials.htm

Provides tutorials on the library catalog, information cycle, and locating business information

Researching a Topic in Four Easy Steps
http://www.library.yale.edu/instruction/topic.html

Uses the following four steps to information literacy: defining the topic, finding out what has already been written on your topic, considering other types of relevant materials research, and locating materials at Yale and beyond

For more information

ACRL Instruction Section
http://www.ala.org/Content/NavigationMenu/ACRL/About_ACRL/Sections/Instruction/IS_Home_Page.htm

Advocates and supports learning, teaching, and research with respect to information literacy in higher education.

Clearinghouse for Library Instruction. Library Orientation Exchange (LOEX)
http://www.emich.edu/public/loex/loex.html

LOEX is a self-supporting, nonprofit educational clearinghouse for materials used in library instruction.

Information Literacy Section. International Federation of Library Associations and Institutions
http://www.ifla.org/VII/rt12/rtued.htm

The primary purpose of the Information Literacy Section is to foster international cooperation in the development of user education in all types of libraries.

Mike Eisenberg and Bob Berkowitz. The Big6
http://www.big6.com

The Big6 approach to teaching information and technology skills includes the following steps: task definition, information-seeking strategies, location of access, use of information, synthesis, and evaluation.

Library Instruction Round Table (LIRT). American Library Association
http://www3.baylor.edu/LIRT

LIRT advocates library instruction as a means for developing competent library and information use as a part of lifelong learning in all types of libraries. Includes a collection of tutorials other libraries have produced.

Smith, Susan Sharpless. 2001. *Web-based instruction: A guide for libraries.* Chicago: ALA.

Webster, Monica R., and Jerome E. Webster. 2001. *How to create online tutorials.* Chicago: ALA.

OBITUARY INDEXES

Because many newspapers do not provide freely accessible access to obituaries, and because patron inquiries regarding obituaries are a constant source of business for libraries, many have made that information accessible via an index. Obituaries are challenging to locate because many variables determine their publication. Some of these variables include the date they are published, the edition they appear in, and whether they appear in the newspaper at all. In some cases, family members decide whether they are published. Newspapers may also print a death notice. Each newspaper differs, but libraries trying to meet this constant demand have, in many cases, produced obituary indexes ranging from the full-text obituaries to indexes of names resulting in the date and page number. Users then request a copy via interlibrary loan. Libraries keeping a print index of obituaries can translate this information into a searchable database with minimal effort by using a number of free and affordable technologies.

Examples

Clark County (Ohio) Public Library
http://guardian.ccpl.lib.oh.us/obits/

Obituaries are indexed from 1926 to the present. Print copies are ordered through the postal mail.

Cleveland Necrology File (Cleveland Public Library)
http://www.cpl.org

According to the web site, the Necrology File is "produced from a microfilmed copy of an alphabetical card file containing local cemetery records and newspaper death notices gathered by the staff of the Cleveland Public Library."

Los Angeles Public Library
http://pubindex.lapl.org/pages/rip.htm

This index allows users to search by name, occupation, date of death, or cause of death (or both) using Boolean operators.

REFERRAL SERVICES

Community referral is a service that libraries offer so that residents have easy access to local resources based on certain needs, for example, listings of English, GED, literacy, and citizenship classes; health care; or resources aimed at a certain population, such as the homeless, unemployed, parents, seniors, and students. A library that offers community referral addresses the need for information related to services provided by community agencies and organizations (Himmel and Wilson 1998). As a service provided by public libraries since the early 1970s, community referral includes three broad subcategories of information: survival or human services information, local information, and citizen action information (Durrance and Pettigrew 2002).

Libraries can offer community referral services by locating, organizing, and providing access to services and resources of local organizations and making this information available on their web sites. Depending on the complexity of the project and the amount of information captured about each organization, a listing can be easily published in HTML or as a PDF document. If there are more than a manageable number of organizations, it may be more appropriate to create a database to handle the information and provide easier access. Many times the library catalog offers the ability to create a community information database that will capture the following information: contact information, description of services, languages spoken, meeting rooms, whether the agency accepts volunteers, and the date the record was last updated.

There are several reasons why libraries should consider offering referral services from their web sites. First, libraries already provide this information, and many have lists of community organizations already documented. Second, it helps libraries build worth in the community as the authors of a very valuable community resource. Depending on the type of community served, and the library's specialty, it may be more appropriate to specialize, for instance, in a legal or medical referral service or other popular topic.

Examples

FIRST: Free Information and Referral System Teleline
http://www.1st.org

A listing of more than 1,000 nonprofit organizations created by the York County Library System (Pa.) and funded by the United Way of York County and the county of York

Monroe County (Ind.) Public Library
http://monroe.lib.in.us/reference/commsrch.html

A database of organizations in Bloomington, Monroe County, and surrounding communities

FIVE

Library Catalogs and Portals

The library catalog, once thought of as solely a discovery tool for library materials, has evolved into a delivery mechanism that offers much more than MARC records for the materials collection and the promise of seamless access to electronic collections and services. Although the catalog has improved in functionality, expectation of its design in a web-based format remain the same. "A good online catalog is obvious: you can see how it works almost immediately; it tells you where you are and how you got there; and, in most cases, it gives you easy ways to find out where you can go from here" (Crawford 1992, 58). Customers and staff want a system that follows sound web standards and principles and allows for easy searching and the ability to interact with the catalog. Recent trends in OPAC development include

- an increasing amount of patron interactivity;
- inclusion of a growing amount of full-text content;
- content enrichment data such as cover art, table of contents, and summaries;
- customization of display screens and search features;
- evolution of the catalog as a portal site;

- integration of the catalog with licensed databases;
- inclusion of virtual reference services;
- compliancy with standards for purposes of interoperability;
- automation of the card application process; and
- e-commerce functionality such as paying fines with credit cards.

As libraries implement more and more of these features through the OPAC, they come closer to offering their customers a web portal as briefly discussed in chapter 2. Many vendors offer libraries the ability to build web portals via their library catalogs through strategic partnerships with outside companies that may provide content or functionality traditionally not available in the catalog. Libraries contract for these services, and via common protocols and standards, the systems are able to communicate with one another. The ability to provide a portal web site allows customers functionality to simultaneously search licensed subscription databases (*see* "Resource Integration" in chapter 6) and other library catalogs. These portal sites provide library customers with seamless access to the print collection, subscription databases, interlibrary loan services, chat reference, and electronic books—all through the library catalog, along with dynamic content such as the *New York Times* bestseller lists, local weather, and news feeds.

"The OPACs themselves were not conceived within a true hypertext environment, but rather they maintain the structure of their original formats, principally MARC, and therefore impede the generation of a structure of nodes and links. Even in cases in which links between authors, subjects, and titles exist, there is no hope for any linking other than mere matching: for example, books of the same author, subject, or similar words in the title" (Ortiz-Repiso and Moscoso 1999). In a very short time we have seen the text-based OPAC move into a new outer shell. The web interface offers substantial changes for user interaction, including pull-down menus instead of command-line searching (Green 1998).

The change in platform has moved us from the keyboard controls to mouse dependency, individual screens versus scrolling through pages, and nonlinear linking with images instead of sequential movements. Web catalogs are based on HTML (HyperText Markup Language), a language that addresses the presentation of information; however, future systems may be based on XML (Extensible Markup Language). XML defines the structure of the information and describes the role of its structured components. It has the promise to work well with the structured MARC record.

A LOOK AT THE COMPETITION

Although libraries welcome use of all sorts, they are particularly concerned in boosting circulation statistics, a key indicator of use. When the OPAC was introduced to the Web, the number of potential customers increased exponentially. Library catalogs were available through the Web, which opened the doors to thousands of libraries and millions of MARC records. That access has provided libraries with the ability to expand their customer base to both library users and nonusers by increasing the availability and usability of the catalog. Library collections, for the most part, are at the very core of the services that libraries provide, so it is troublesome that the catalog is simply a link from the home page and not afforded the importance that it deserves. Take, for example, online bookstores, whose core business includes selling books in a variety of formats, including print, audio, DVD, videos, music, and more. They often link to events and programs being offered in local stores, such as book discussion and writing groups, children's story times, and craft programs. Although we share some common service and collection points, a comparison of a library web site and a bookstore site show marked differences. For example, when logging on to Barnes and Noble's web site (http://www.bn.com), the user is presented with the following items:

Pop-up window that changes daily

Two navigation bars:

> *Primary:* browse books, what's new, best-sellers, coming soon, recommended, book clubs

> *Secondary:* meet the writers, audio books, new and used textbooks, business and technical books, children's books, DVD and video, music, used and out-of-print books, half-price books, online courses

Free e-mail alerts: "We'll e-mail you when your favorite books, DVD, and music are released!"

The Barnes and Noble web site uses multiple access points to the same web pages. By using redundant links with different textual cues, the site caters to a variety of different users who may click on a link because it appeals to them. For example, the following phrases are used to arrive at the same page:

Barnes & Noble University and Online Courses

Used & Out of Print Books and "Buying Used Books Just Got Easier"

Browse Books and "Browse. Need Help Finding the Right Book?"

Some of the differences that appear almost immediately are the heavy use of book cover art, the option to browse the collection, and such e-commerce components as shopping cart checkout, shipping information, and wish lists. Also, one would notice the jargon that appears to dominate library catalogs. "It frequently happens that OPAC users are confronted with a vocabulary different from the usage in common language, such as 'Boolean operators,' 'Authorities,' 'MARC,' and 'ISBD'" (Ortiz-Repiso and Moscoso 1999). Perhaps in the future, the library catalog will be the central focus of the library web site, but for the many libraries who have not implemented library web portals, it currently remains a link off of the home page alongside information such as events and programs, planning documents, and job advertisements.

CUSTOMIZING THE CATALOG

Crawford describes the library-defined catalog accurately when he writes that "within the next few years, even the smallest library will have the luxury and the burden those university libraries have that built their own online catalogs have had for some time." He continues, "Naturally, you will be able to use the vendor defaults . . . but you will have increasing flexibility to move beyond those defaults" (Crawford 1992, 2). Crawford's statements were, of course, describing the web-based catalog. As HTML was used to create the graphical user interface, vendors offered the ability of customization for such features as text size, font style, inserting graphics, manipulation of search screens, bibliographic displays, and result screens.

As visitors move from library web page to library catalog, they should experience few, if any, cues that they have moved to a new site. Many times when researchers make the jump from web page to catalog, they are forwarded to a design entirely different from that of the library's, leaving users to wonder if they are still at the library's web site at all. Because web catalogs are based in HTML, they can be edited, and libraries should strive to maintain the look and feel of the library's web site and provide a smooth transition from library web site to library catalog.

Other tips follow:

Include the library logo and same type of images used on the web site.

Create images depicting different material formats to replace those supplied by the vendor.

The main navigation bar of the library web site should be visible on the library catalog.

Help files must be edited to reflect any customization made.

Document all customization so it may be duplicated in the non-English version of the catalog.

If the library maintains a catalog in another language besides English, then any customization and upgrades would have to be applied to each log-in. Help files should mirror any customization the library implements. Additionally, libraries may create different profiles of the catalog for each branch location. Conrad and Lessner suggest that different log-ins didn't pose a problem for the users within libraries because they were able to embed log-in information in the URL and set it as the browser's home page. That way, library staff did not have to remember which way a station should be logged in (2002).

"One of the difficulties is that there are many different kinds of the users of Web-based OPACs according to a number of variables, such as age, gender, educational status, library and computer experience as well as tasks and goals" (Kim et al. 1999, 83). These user characteristics also have categories, as explained by Kim and others, that are short term, long term, and that change through time.

Customizing Search Screens

Prior to the proliferation of the web-based OPAC, literature suggests giving patrons no more than nine choices per screen (Crawford 1992). A look at some of the most popular web sites shows, however, that visitors often have more than fifty links from which to choose. Web surfers are accustomed to many choices; yet once a searcher has entered the library catalog, the choices decrease significantly. The main navigation bar usually remains, along with links and options within the catalog. Libraries normally present users with an easy search screen that may default to a keyword search unless a search by author or title is selected. When user decisions are fewer, fewer choices may limit the structure of the queries and what they can accomplish (Green 1998). Universities, whose students and faculty may have more advanced searching needs, usually provide users with more sophisticated search screens up front by offering them the following ways to search: title, keyword, subject, author, journal, journal title, call number or other numbers, course reserves by course, and course reserves by instructor. Public libraries generally offer limited search options on search entry screens with a link to more advanced options.

Bibliographic Displays

Libraries have continually customized the look of the brief record list and the full bibliographic display. A question that libraries grapple with is determining what items are important to the user. For example, when viewing the brief record, should users be presented with the title, author, and date of publication? Library staff should determine what bibliographic elements are most necessary to display in order for searchers to decide whether to click on the item for more information.

Once patrons arrive at the full bibliographic record, they need information that will help them determine whether to request the item. The design of this screen is conditional upon its content and the presentation of the information. What items of the bibliographic record should appear "above the fold" so that users do not have to scroll down to get the information that the majority of users would need to know? Figure 5.1 outlines the difference between brief record displays in an online bookstore, a public library OPAC, and a university catalog.

The following items appear in a book's brief record on Amazon.com:	The following items appear in a book's brief record on the Yale University Library Catalog (http://orbis.library.yale.edu):	The following items appear in a book's brief record on the Flagstaff-Coconino (Ariz.) Public Library Catalog (http://www.flagstaffpubliclibrary.org):
Title of the book (this is the link to the full record)	Check box to mark record	Entry number
Image of the book jacket (with a "look inside" graphic)	Entry number (this is the link to the full record)	Graphic with the words "Full Detail" (this is the link to the full record)
Author	Title	Check box to "keep" item
Date of publication	Author	Call number
Customer rating	Full title	Title
Edition	Imprint	Author
Shipping information	Location	Availability
List price	Call number	Date of publication
Buy-new price	Status	Graphics indicating a review, summary, and sample chapter
In-store pickup price		Cover art

Figure 5.1 Comparing Brief Records

One of the main differences, outside of the e-commerce functionality of the online bookstore, is the placement of the link to go to the full record display.

A MATTER OF SEMANTICS: LABELING FOR ACCESS

Libraries continually strive to use labels that are meaningful to customers and have always had difficulty translating library terminology into words and phrases that users understand. Many academic libraries give their catalogs a name (Orbis at Yale University, Melvyl at University of California Libraries, CONSULS at Connecticut State University Library System) that may not necessarily describe the link accurately. Some libraries create a link labeled "Online Catalog" on their web sites, a term the profession has used ever since computers were introduced to paper-based card catalogs. If users are already online, then the use of the word *online* is redundant.

Other libraries are using words to describe what you find in the library catalog. In *Terms Found on Usability-Tested Library Home Pages* (Kupersmith 2002), several university libraries reported using the following tested phrases besides "library catalog": "what we own," "catalog of books & more," and "how do I find a book." There exists an ongoing discussion in the web librarian community regarding using the library catalog as a noun or action word ("catalog" versus "find a book") on the library web site. Furthermore, use of the phrase "Full Record," which leads OPAC users to the full bibliographic record, may mean to a nonlibrary user that the book is in use. In one case, the mental model that this student brought was that of an object he wanted to reserve or a class he wanted to take. To him, that book was full—or unavailable (Green 1998).

Interestingly, online bookstores do not use any term to identify their catalogs. The search for materials is assumed by the users by a simple text box labeled "Search" or "Browse." Additionally, customers move to the full record simply by clicking on the link from the title of the book. As libraries begin labeling buttons and links within the catalog, it may be important to test changes as they are implemented using a focus group.

CONTENT ENRICHMENT

Content enrichment materials are added to library catalogs so that users can find more information about materials and, as a result, become more engaged with the catalog. The content available extends and supplements MARC information. This feature can be contracted directly from its source or, in some cases, through strategic alliances that an ILS vendor has established. A result of adding features and more information to the catalog is that more people are going to be using the system for longer periods of time (Crawford 1992), especially because they have the ability to access the catalog from the comfort of their homes.

Content enrichment includes the following types of materials:

Full-text reviews

Annotations

Tables of contents

First chapters

Excerpts

Author notes

Book jacket images

Series information

Summaries

Once the link is set up from the catalog, updates are seamlessly incorporated into new MARC records. If the content elements are added at a later date, the connection to those materials is made without library intervention.

EXTERNAL WEB SITES: IMPLICATIONS FOR THE LIBRARY WEB SITE AND CATALOG

One of the characteristics of the Web is the ability for one web site to link to another. Librarians especially find the task of locating, evaluating, collecting, and organizing web sites a function of collection development. Libraries can acquire links from staff, the public, students, or faculty members. They may also purchase the MARC records of web sites for inclusion into the catalog.

Although the links are free, including and maintaining links to external web sites through the library's web site and catalog is not. "While one web site may occupy a limited amount of a staff member's time in identifying, annotating, and marking up, the accumulation of sites can begin to develop real costs" (Latham 2002, 21). In addition to Latham's concerns regarding costs, libraries must also address policy issues (*see* chapter 1) and procedural issues such as (1) responsibility for finding, annotating, updating, and weeding links and (2) web site maintenance, including frequency of updates and programming time, if applicable.

There exists a duplication of efforts when libraries purchase MARC records of web sites for upload into the catalog while reference librarians spend time choosing, evaluating, categorizing, and placing web sites on the library web site. One would think that if the web sites are worth linking to from the library web site, then they would be worth the staff time to enter into the catalog. However, this defeats the purpose of purchasing the records from a vendor. One would imagine that if the library purchases MARC records of web sites, then librarians should have the ability to (1) add new web sites not currently in the catalog and (2) create links from the web site that dynamically post them on the web site.

Selection Criteria

A clearly written and well-researched policy will help to support the rationale for inclusion of free web sites. Libraries should create a process for selecting free web resources as well as for maintaining them. The problems associated with the Web, including "inconsistent quality among web sites, and the disappearance of their URLs resulting in the dreaded 404 message" (Porter and Bayard 1999, 390), may have diminished since the shakedown of the dot-com industry occurring shortly after 2000. Librarians also rate web sites according to selection criteria that have developed out of literature created by information literacy documents from academic librarians like Hope Tillman, whose publication "Evaluating Quality on the Net" (2003) was first used by librarians as a basis to develop selection criteria. Selection criteria for web sites should include the following guidelines:

Authority. Is the author of the material considered an authority in the subject area? Is the authoring agent the most appropriate sponsor of the information? How stable is the author and will this site be available in the future? Is there a link to contact the author or agency?

Accuracy and Objectivity. Is the information correct? Are other sources referenced? If the information is produced from a print source, it should be checked against the original and not be altered in any way. Does the information presented show bias or are all points of an issue covered? Does the author have anything to gain or lose within the scope of the topics covered?

Accessibility. How fast does the page load? Are plug-ins or additional software needed to access files? And, if so, is this clearly stated, with a link to the site where you can obtain the software? Are the browser requirements listed and does a visitor need the most current graphical browser to view the site properly? Can this site be accessed on all library computers?

Design. Does the design of the page complement the user experience? Are there unnecessary animation or large graphics that hinder access to the content? Can one easily print the screen or are alternative printer-friendly pages available where appropriate?

Coverage and Currency. Is the content local? Does it present information not found elsewhere? Does the subject reflect common information inquiries? Is the material offered comprehensive or is there information lacking? Is the page or site kept current and are last revision dates printed on content pages?

Editorial Concerns. Is the writing level appropriate for the intended audience? Is the page free of grammatical errors? Does dynamic content follow the same editorial scrutiny from the rest of the site?

Privacy Issues. Does the site ask for personal information and, if so, does it include privacy statements? A link to the site's policy statement should be placed near forms or text boxes asking patrons for personal information.

Additional criteria for the selection of external links follow:

Children's sites must be in compliance with the Children's Online Privacy Protection Act.

Sites for seniors should adhere to design principles for readers with low vision.

Sites should be accessible using the library's computer.

Bibliographers' Sources

Combing through the Internet for new web sites can be extremely time-consuming, given the often superfluous nature of the Internet. Estimates from the Web Characterization Project (WCP) place the size of the public Web at 3,080,000 sites in June 2002 (OCLC 2002). There are several sources for free and fee-based lists of worthwhile web sites. Current awareness tools such as newsletters are used to identify web sites or enhancements to existing web sites. Libraries can also purchase fully cataloged quality web sites from a variety of vendors. Companies offering this service typically provide Library of Congress Subject Headings and classification numbers, Dewey classification numbers, and annotations describing the web site in MARC format. Companies also provide updates to report changes to the records. Libraries may also choose to purchase a collection of web sites from a vendor and then have staff monitor the free sources for new available sites. Vendors offer cataloged web sites in MARC format that conform to AACR2. They normally include annotations, LC subject headings, LC and Dewey call numbers, and the URL in the 856 field. For company listings, *see* appendix B.

Presentation

Whether providing access to external links from web pages or from the catalog, there exist a variety of design and usability issues. The URL for a web document resides in the 856 field of a MARC record. Web users will intuitively click on the title of the resource to get more information about it. If the 856 field does not display near the title, users may not understand that they can actually access the document online. Also, the ability to request a title must be disabled when the user retrieves full-text electronic resources that display in the catalog.

When providing outbound links from web pages, some libraries include an exit page that informs visitors that they are leaving the library web site. According to usability expert Jakob Nielsen, this practice is not suggested (2000). In addition, Nielsen states that opening a new browser to indicate the visitor is going to an external site is not recommended. Once a new window opens, the back button is no longer functional in the new browser. Because users are normally trained to navigate with the back and forward buttons, they are lost. A user who tries to return to the origin will be confused by a grayed-out text button. Nielsen suggests using the design of the links to differentiate internal from external links.

A CASE STUDY

Westerville (Ohio) Public Library uses Innovative Interfaces to provide a customized catalog (http://catalog.wpl.lib.oh.us) to their patrons and is the 2003 recipient of the most innovative web OPAC award from that same company. Westerville Public Library is a one-branch facility, although you would not know it from its state-of-the-art web site, and has created the following OPAC features:

- A scoping feature markets a segment of the collection by the type of material. Scopes include access to materials in adult and youth services, media services, and sites on the Internet.
- Use of color selections, custom graphics, and customized header and footer navigation bars contribute to the overall design, which provides a seamless experience for users as they move from library web site to library catalog.
- MetaFind allows visitors to search multiple resources—such as the catalog, search engines, image search engines, magazines, and newspapers.
- The brief citation browse display provides users with quick access to the information most important.

A custom graphic can be created when the book cover art is not available. Patrons view a graphic with the following title: "The Dog Ate the Cover."

In addition, functionality such as e-mail notification sign-up, online card registration, a customized help section, and the ability to mark records and place them in a shopping cart to either view or e-mail is offered.

For more information

Westerville (Ohio) Public Library

http://www.westervillelibrary.org/iii/be-innovative.htm

Westerville staff provide an in-depth description of the various customizations made to the library catalog.

SIX

Licensed Databases and Electronic Books

As vendors transfer data from print to electronic format, libraries are challenged to provide users with easy access to these materials. When the distribution of information transferred from CD-ROMs to the Web, libraries could no longer provide access to the products through stand-alone computers not connected to the Internet. Accessing the web-based subscription databases required a connection to the Internet, and without remote access, libraries had to provide the access points for patrons to use the databases. Public librarians found that the majority of patrons who did not have Internet access from home were using library computers for Internet access, however, not for research purposes. Many libraries solved the problem by designating certain terminals for catalog and database use only. Academic libraries also have several configurations in their facilities, such as terminals that can only access the library catalog, research databases, and production software. Eventually, vendors allowed remote access to databases when libraries could provide authentication through library cards or other methods. This was clearly a boon for libraries. Libraries no longer had to ensure that their library computers were the only access points to these valuable resources. Their visitors could now access library materials through any computer that was connected to the Web. Although the Web as a medium for delivery of information has proven advantages over earlier formats (print, microfilm, CD-ROM), clearly libraries continue to face challenges in making these resources accessible.

Libraries acquire electronic resources by many means, including purchasing them through their own budgets, through cooperatives, and through state consortia. Statewide database purchases have allowed libraries access to databases that they may not have been able to afford on their own, thus freeing up some money to allow libraries to buy access to additional databases. Some vendors may offer libraries a free database for a year for promotional purposes. Vendors may also offer libraries online access to journals when they subscribe to the print version of the same title. Many of the challenges that libraries face are because of the sheer quantity of web-based subscriptions that are available. Many libraries have created "databases of databases" that help them keep track of vendor contacts (both sale and technical), cost, renewal dates, instructions on accessing statistics, and URLs to access the database in an effort to help manage the subscriptions.

RESEARCH DATABASES AND ELECTRONIC JOURNALS

Placement and Presentation

Librarians began to use the phrase "electronic resources" or "online databases" to differentiate subscription databases from their print and CD-ROM counterparts. Print journals became electronic journals. Furthermore, many of the magazine and newspaper databases began to include additional content such as images, government publications, investment reports, poems, encyclopedias, and web sites. There are also other formats and topics to consider, such as test preparation software, reader's advisory tools, and electronic books.

Unfortunately, some vendors have titled databases in a manner that does not promote awareness and understanding of these resources. Visitors would not know the content of the databases simply by the title but would have to read a description. Libraries could even be the recipients of a competing product with the same title (for example, a series titled Professional Development Collection is available from both EBSCO and Gale) if they purchased one and received the other through a statewide purchase. Libraries face challenges on how to present the databases in a meaningful way so that users can understand their value and how they differ from free web sites. Subscription databases provide information that is placed under the scrutiny of an editorial process, whereas web sites may be constructed by anyone with the resources to post it to the Internet.

A Link from the Home Page

A link to subscription databases should be prominently displayed on the library home page, not only because of their value, but partly because these resources may represent a large percentage of the materials budget. Certainly the amount of money that is spent on electronic databases warrants a link from the home page. If patrons cannot find the databases, they will not access them. Kupersmith's *Terms Found on Usability-Tested Library Home Pages* recorded the following statement, which was the outcome of a usability study at the University of Arizona: "If students have no idea why or when they should use an index, they will not choose a link labeled *Index*, no matter how well designed the web page is." The majority of the students tend to use the following specific terms (*articles, journals, magazines,* and *newspapers*) instead of the more general ones (*index, resources,* and *databases*) (Kupersmith 2002); however, it is certainly possible to use multiple access points to the information.

Tabs

Librarians have experimented with a variety of ways to provide access to this group of resources spanning many topics and formats. One way that works well is the use of tabs (*see* figure 6.1), a design technique popularized by sites like Amazon.com and Barnesandnoble.com.

Customization

Researchers are normally unfamiliar with the library's relationship with third-party vendors; however, most users realize they have linked to another site because the design of the screen changes. Vendors have allowed libraries to display their logos within the screens, and normally the logo links back to the library web page. In addition, vendors may also allow libraries to insert a link to the live reference service, if available, so that library patrons are not sending questions blindly to the vendor's customer or technical service staff. Customization within vendor databases may include the ability to change search screens and results page defaults and use different language interfaces.

Functionality

Database vendors offer a wide range of functionality; however, each database warrants special consideration depending on its content, for example, the option to search by occupation or ethnicity in a biographical database. The following list represents some of the most common functions in a database:

Figure 6.1 Databases by Tabs, Chicago (Ill.) Public Library. The Chicago Public Library (http://www.chipublib.org) uses three tabs to guide users to the most appropriate database.

Ability to limit searches by date, language, journal, local holdings, and full-text content

Browsing options

Inclusion of authority files for subjects, authors, and journals

Field searching by title, date, and author

Sorting results and marking records

Output options, including print, download, e-mail, and the display of printer-friendly pages

Search features such as Boolean, proximity, and truncation

Authentication and Access

Web users are inundated with the amount of account numbers, user names, and passwords from a range of web sites that they visit. If patrons are located in the library, the most common way to authenticate use of licensed databases is through IP (Internet Protocol) authentication. IP addresses identify computers on the Internet, and the IP range includes all computers within a library building or multibranch system. The library supplies the IP range to the vendor so that when a library patron tries to access the database from a library computer, he or she is automatically allowed access. Remote access to databases involves a more sophisticated authentication scheme because visitors have to prove who they are before they can access licensed content. Remote authentication schemes include the use of proxy servers and vendor recognition of referring URLs so that once the library authenticates the patron, the vendor allows access so long as the patron is coming from a specific page. The use of a proxy server may require that users adjust their settings in their web browsers by adding the proxy server's IP address and port settings; however, this may place additional workload on the server should patrons forget to disable it (Breeding 2001). Additional schemes for encryption of information include Secure Sockets Layer (SSL), used for sending encrypted information over the Internet, such as password or credit card information, and providing necessary proof that user are who they say they are; digital certificates, software-based IDs that use encryption to confirm a user's identify; and smart cards, which embed a small chip in a card that allows storage of information (Guenther 2003). Third-party software also helps libraries ensure that they are providing secure remote access.

When accessing library web site resources, visitors expect to do so with one user name and password. Confusion and frustration arise when visitors are asked to continually authenticate throughout their visit to third-party sites, including a different authentication system for the library catalog. Furthermore, remote access patrons on some web sites are required to click on a link specifically labeled "home access." Once users are authenticated, some vendors may require the users to create an account with them. Unfortunately, too many barriers exist between library users and subscription databases.

Levels of access are dependent upon products, vendors, contracts, and patron residency. The following variables included in vendor contracts establish the baseline level of access:

Unlimited remote access

Library use only

Branch-specific access

Limit on number of simultaneous users

It may also be necessary to distinguish between patron types based on residency or university status. For instance, many libraries offer statewide library cards, and some universities offer community and alumni library cards. Public libraries that issue statewide library cards to users may have to block access to databases that are library purchased while allowing all cardholders into the state- and consortium-purchased databases. Universities may have to authenticate students enrolled in certain programs instead of allowing full-campus access.

Authentication must be able to accomplish the following tasks:

Provide seamless access to all library and vendor resources 24/7 regardless if the catalog is down

Require log-in once, with the option for users to stay logged in until they log off

Determine level of access the user gets based on patron status

Allow users to authenticate with user names and passwords they create

Send PIN or authentication information via e-mail if a patron forgets it

Resource Integration

As libraries continue to add more and more licensed databases and the trend toward the availability of more full-text content continues, libraries must find a way to make the patron's search easier. Resource integration software offers researchers an integrated gateway with one convenient search interface for online database searching. The software solves many problems previously discussed in this chapter. Various names for this functionality are "broadcast searching," "cross-domain searching," and "information portal" (Curtis 2002, 54). This is particularly important as libraries continue to supply an increasing amount of content in an unmediated environment.

This concept is very similar to that of Dialindex (File 411), a database offered by Dialog (http://www.dialog.com), which is designed to identify the most relevant databases of the hundreds that this company offers. Resource integration software allows users to search the online catalog, full-text magazine and newspaper databases, encyclopedias, and reference databases simultaneously. Otherwise, researchers have to scroll through a list of databases to determine which one is most relevant to their search.

Some vendors have solved this problem by providing one interface for all or most of their products (e.g., EBSCOhost from EBSCO); however, for the most part, users leave the library web site and are expected to learn how to search and find materials in each database. If staff are overwhelmed by determining which database is most appropriate for the research question, then we can only assume patrons are also confused. Webmasters can retrieve a list of words and phrases input by users into the web site's search engine. Many times visitors input words describing keywords and subjects of the information they are looking for, not necessarily for information on the library's web site. This in itself is proof that this software turns an often cumbersome quest for information into a very intuitive one by searching subscription databases, the library catalog, and even other web sites and search engines simultaneously. Some ILS vendors have developed strategic partnerships with resource integration software vendors and allow customers to search all of these resources simultaneously through the OPAC. *See* chapter 5 for information about portal web sites.

Expecting researchers to choose the appropriate database, quite possibly among one hundred of them, is similar to the job of the reference librarian, matching resource with query. When patrons access collections via the web site, the onus of matching the appropriate resource with the question falls on the patrons. When someone searches in Google, he or she retrieves a variety of formats, such as multimedia, HTML, PDF, and Microsoft's PowerPoint, Excel, Word, and Access database files. Library visitors should not have to seek out a specific format such as a government document or an electronic book, for that matter. Like in Google, their search on the library's web site should retrieve all library materials regardless of format and location, including materials in the library catalog.

Selecting Targets and Scoping

Libraries must choose targets for inclusion in the search. Some vendors require that the targets be Z39.50 compliant. Z39.50 is an American National Standard that defines a protocol for computer-to-computer information retrieval. Most subscription-based services that libraries purchase are Z39.50 compliant; however, products that can search outside of the Z39.50 standard allow the flexibility to include additional resources such as web sites or locally produced databases. Libraries may even choose to include popular search engines as targets so that users do not have to leave the library's web site for further research.

The presentation of the information is also important. Some software may allow scoping, the grouping together of databases by subject. So, for example, all of a library's business resources can be searched simultaneously. In addition to subject categories, libraries can also opt to group age-appropriate databases in one category.

So Much to Gain, but What Do We Lose?

Librarians are concerned that patrons will not have access to the full search capabilities of the library catalog or other library databases by diluting functionality to the lowest common denominator, a keyword search. Although this may be true, it's important to realize that this type of software is an awareness tool that allows patrons to become more familiar with each database before delving into each database for more advanced searching. It would be impossible to provide some of the advanced search capabilities that are unique to some of the databases (such as the example used above describing a search by occupation or ethnicity in a biographical database). Its strength is not in the potency of the search, but its ability to designate the most appropriate resource for the patron's query while still allowing direct access to search the databases individually. Patrons are inundated with information, and as unmediated searching and remote visits to the library increase, resource integration software allows us to offer easy access to a treasure trove of information not found elsewhere on the Internet.

Additional concerns include the amount of results retrieved and the order in which they are displayed. Ideally, the most relevant results should be displayed first. The ability to choose which target results are listed first, not based on the fastest response time, but by library or patron preference, or relevancy would offer the best solution. King County Library System uses tabs to organize results (*see* figure 6.2).

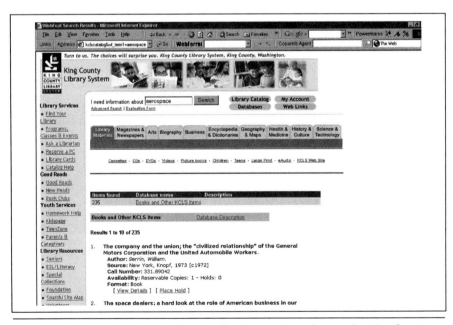

Figure 6.2 Resource Integration, King County (Wash.) Library System. The King County Library System (http://www.kcls.org) has ordered results to be displayed on different web pages organized by tabs.

Full-Text Serials

Although access to full-text periodicals has grown, at the same time aggregators have discontinued or added rights to publications. Additionally, certain periodicals are embargoed (the time period from print publication to when they are available online). This delays the date they actually appear in the database. Last, the results of *The New York Times v. Tasini* have caused publishers to remove articles written by freelance writers for years prior to the mid-1990s, when electronic rights were not considered in contracts. It is uncertain how much content has been removed from the databases; however, librarians and researchers should be aware that this chasm in coverage exists.

Many vendors maintain full-title lists on their web sites that staff can use to verify access (index, abstracts, full text) to particular periodicals and to check local holdings. Libraries may also obtain MARC records for the journals and download them to the library catalog; however, this provides a two-step method to determine if the library has access to a magazine. Visitors to the web site in search of an article may find it difficult to find a list of magazines to which the library subscribes. Access and authentication barriers previously discussed exist for these visitors, too.

With access to databases from various vendors and the discontinuation and addition of full-text content, even library staff are unable to quickly find a way to gain access to the resources available. Many resources remain underutilized and quite possibly generate erroneous interlibrary loan requests. How can libraries connect patrons with the vast amount of information located in aggregated databases? Because of the shifting nature of these holdings, frequent updating is necessary, making the task of keeping up with changes nearly impossible for a library to manage on its own. Fortunately, services exist that offer a consolidated list of online full-text magazine and newspaper holdings to which libraries subscribe. Print and microfiche holdings can be included if the library provides the information to the vendor. Frequency of updates range from weekly to bimonthly to quarterly.

Links from journal titles displayed on the library web site may take researchers directly to the full text of the journal title or they will be linked to the database search page. Proxy server prefixes and customized URLs can be incorporated into the linked title list so that users are prompted for the appropriate access information. Full-text journal lists can be delivered to libraries in many formats, including Microsoft Excel, comma delimited, HTML, XML, MARC, or PDF. Libraries can easily present them by title or offer their visitors the ability to search by journal title or keyword. The amount of staff time needed to implement this service includes time spent preparing a list of print and microfiche holdings and the development of a search interface.

In addition to organizing full-text serial lists, technologies exist that can boost usage of your online journal collection. If a library subscribes to multiple vendor databases, a journal may be indexed in one database and available in full text in another. Linking technology allows linking between databases, even from different vendors. Caplan outlines several scenarios involving reference linking (2001, 16):

> You are searching an online index to the literature in your discipline. In your retrieval list there are a number of entries containing links that say "click here to see this article." You click one, and the article appears in your browser.

> You are reading an electronic journal article. At the end of the article is a section labeled "References," followed by a list of works cited by the author. Some of the citations have the link "Article Full Text." You click, and the cited article appears in your browser.

> A colleague sends you an e-mail citing a work she thinks you should read. The note contains a link. You click, and a copy of the work appears in your browser.

Caplan explains that the building blocks of these technologies include identifiers (identifies the content) and resolvers (associates identifiers with locations). The most popular identifier is the Digital Object Identifier (DOI). Publishers submit each DOI with a corresponding URL to the International DOI Foundation (2001). Furthermore, Grogg and Ferguson discuss the inclusion of local print holdings, interlibrary loan, and document delivery options: "How can libraries and information centers offer one link, from any source (database, OPAC, e-journal subscription at publisher's web site), to any appropriate other source (full text, print holdings, other e-journal subscriptions, ILL, document delivery)? Libraries and information centers can offer such dynamic linking through context-sensitive linking by the rather elegant inclusion of a linking technology known as the OpenURL" (2003, 26). (OpenURL is discussed below.)

The basic premise behind these services is to increase accessibility to and awareness and usage of the library's electronic databases as well as to aid in collection development and the efficiency of services like interlibrary loan and document delivery. It is clear, however, that if libraries intend to continue purchasing online databases, especially if they are replacing print and microfilm formats with electronic access, they need an effective way to keep up with the changes inherent in an electronic environment as well as the content in context to user searches.

Linking Glossary (EBSCO)

CrossRef

A publisher-sponsored organization that acts as a registry for articles available online. Publishers register their articles with CrossRef by submitting the article metadata, the DOI, and the URL to the article. CrossRef operates a proxy server that allows a DOI to be used as a link to an article. CrossRef also operates lookup services for DOIs and metadata.

Digital Object Identifier (DOI)

A unique and persistent identifier for an article. DOIs are registered with CrossRef along with the URL to the article. The DOI can be submitted to a proxy server (http://dx.doi.org/<DOI>) as a link, and the user is redirected to the article.

Item Level Links

Most databases allow the end user to locate items (such as articles, books, documents, etc.) on a particular topic. Links to either the full text of an item or to other resources related or relevant to the item are referred to as item level links.

Link Resolver

A link server. A web-based application that accepts item information (normally citation data formatted according to OpenURL standard; *see* below) as URL parameters and attempts to locate relevant and context-sensitive links for the item described. The link resolver presents the user with a list of appropriate links.

OpenURL

A definition and syntax for describing an item (e.g., metadata elements) on a URL. Used primarily for use with link resolvers. OpenURL, which has growing industry adoption, is currently in the process of being made a national standard.

Examples

Cuyahoga County (Ohio) Public Library
http://www.cuyahogalibrary.org; select Research, Databases
Visitors can browse by serial title.

The Queens Borough (N.Y.) Public Library
http://www.queenslibrary.org; select Research
Users can search by title and ISSN.

For more information

Caplan, Priscilla L. 2001. A lesson in linking. *Library Journal netConnect* (fall): 16–18.

Curtis, Donnelyn, and Paoshan Yue. 2002. Acquiring and managing electronic journals. *ERIC Digest* (November). EDO-IR-2002-07. Also available at http://www.ericit.org/digests/EDO-IR-2002-07.shtml.

ELECTRONIC BOOKS

An electronic book, also called an e-book, is a "hand-held electronic device on which the text of a book can be read. Also: a book whose text is available in an electronic format for reading on such a device or on a computer screen; a book whose text is available only or primarily on the Internet" (Oxford 2000). The concept of the e-book began more than thirty years ago, in 1971, with the start of Project Gutenberg, a project to digitize thousands of copyright-free books (Garner, Horwood, and Sullivan 2001). Although electronic books received a lukewarm reception from readers, there is still the promise that electronic books offer, one that is still in development. Vendors have made great strides with help from the library profession and the book publishing industry, but issues remain unsolved with regard to compatibility of e-book publishers, reading devices, platform, and digital rights management. Additionally, librarians are still uncertain about user acceptance of the format. Several organizations are involved in the future of electronic books, such as the National Institute of Standards and Technology (NIST), which began sponsoring conferences for the format in 1998. NIST involved "creating a neutral meeting ground for publishers, manufacturers, and authors" (NIST 2003).

What Makes E-books So Great and So Bad

Electronic books hold a great deal of promise for the publishing industry. E-books are available 24/7 from any computer with Internet access. E-books have such special features as search capabilities and the ability to bookmark, write notes, and highlight text. Last, they are portable (depending on the vendor), and readers are able to download them to PDAs (personal digital assistants) to read offline. E-books do not have to be processed or handled by staff for checkout, renewal, or reshelving. Readers do not have to pay fines because e-books are automatically returned.

Electronic books also pose a great deal of challenges for the publishing industry, such as securing copyright-protected materials, and, unfortunately, this has placed many restrictions on their functionality and availability. Vendors within the industry are beginning to learn how to limit potential abuse inherent to this format; however, this creates obstacles for library patrons, including the ability to print, download, and read offline. Librarians have also been surprised to learn that if a patron has an e-book checked out to him or her, unless the library purchases more than one copy, other users who attempt to check the book out will be unable to do so. E-book collections are unlike research databases, which may have unlimited simultaneous access.

Format

E-books are available in a variety of formats; however, the web-based format is so attractive because users need only a computer and a web browser to view the book. Unfortunately, the portability of e-books is one of its main attractions, and users may want the ability to download the book to their PDAs. If the vendor allows readers to download e-books to PDAs, then libraries must determine the software that the vendor supports.

There are multiple manufacturers of PDAs; currently, the two main platforms, or operating systems, are Palm and Pocket PC. At this time, the most popular viewing software are Adobe Ebook Reader, Microsoft Reader, Palm Reader, and Mobipocket Reader. For a complete table of devices, readers, and platforms, *see* "Which format should I choose," located at http://www.ebooks. com. Select Help, then FAQs.

E-book vendors also provide library customers with MARC records for inclusion into the library catalog. This is critical if you want patrons to find the e-books. Visitors to the library may not specifically set out looking for e-books; however, they may find them in a subject search while using the catalog. Although the link to the e-book appears in the 856 field, when displayed in the full bibliographic record, it may not be obvious to users that the record represents a full-text online book. Some customization of the bibliographic display may be necessary.

Implications for Libraries

Electronic books may solve problems librarians encounter with items that experience high demand, such as electronic reserves, as well as high-theft items like books on witchcraft and Cliffs notes. Advantages include the following: items cannot be stolen, hidden, or vandalized; reshelving time and loans are eliminated; items are available 24/7; and loan returns are automatic (Garner, Horwood, and Sullivan 2001). E-books require a substantial investment because libraries must pay for title acquisition and a setup or annual access fee. When reviewing the purchase of e-books, libraries must determine how selecting among the various e-book vendors affects the implementation and usage of the collection. It may be difficult to invest in a variety of vendor products because functionality may differ from each vendor. All e-book vendors manage their collections differently and include varying levels of functionality. Clearly, the development of standards and digital rights management will continue to play an important role in the electronic book industry.

SEVEN

Reader Services

T he power of technology allows librarians to promote leisure reading by offering reader's advisory (RA) services through the library's web site. Libraries offer a wide array and varying degrees of RA services in their buildings, some of which transfer online easily and some of which require a bit more effort. Some libraries have created entire sites dedicated to reading, while others have created a page of external links, bookmarks for kids to color, and web pages promoting author visits. In a study of RA web sites, the following items were prevalent: genre book lists, a degree of interactivity, and links to external web sites (Kelly 2000). Libraries also offer access to RA subscription databases.

As explained in *Talking with Readers: A Workbook for Readers' Advisory*, RA generally consists of a mixture of passive and active strategies. Passive strategies do not involve direct patron contact and consist of creating book lists, displays, and shelving arrangements. Active strategies include those involving person-to-person contact such as leading a book discussion group or sponsoring an author visit (EBSCO 2000).

Passive strategies libraries can implement through the Web include creating reading lists and links to external RA sites of interest, offering subscription-based RA tools and reviews written by staff, and promoting book discussion groups and author visits. Active strategies for content creation on a library RA page include involving readers in the creation of reviews, setting up the online interaction of readers and authors, allowing readers to suggest titles for purchase, and offering online book discussions.

Web content and services cannot live exclusively on the web site without relation to the library's existing RA services. Readers expect to interact with staff about reading, and they expect staff who are competent about the latest titles, authors, old favorites, and the use of the library web site and online tools. It is important for libraries to continue to train staff in the craft of RA interviews. It is important for staff to be readers and to employ the expertise of the many reference books and online RA tools that can help them guide readers to their next book.

Last, and covered in more depth in chapter 5, a reader-centered library catalog is crucial. The ease with which a reader can access the collection and the functionality of the catalog can truly enhance a patron's reading experience. Some features that readers generally request are the ability to save a list of materials they have read; the ability to create annotations of their reading experience; the ability to create lists that can be shared with others, such as the "Listmania" function found in Amazon.com; and the ability to find out how long they will have to wait for a book. Content enrichment materials such as book cover art, tables of contents, and reviews have also greatly increased the appeal of library catalogs.

Some library catalogs offer features that net-savvy patrons are already accustomed to, such as results ranked by relevancy, a shopping cart feature, and hot links to What Others Are Reading, More by This Author, and More Like This. Libraries add these features to their web sites for increased functionality, content, and marketing appeal. Libraries should put great emphasis on the library catalog as it is the portal to their collections and one readers rely on to provide access to their reading materials.

Libraries have many possibilities to explore when delivering RA services via the Internet and can choose to offer both active and passive services for adult and youth readers. Libraries with well-established RA services will find it much easier to transfer these services to the Web because the majority of the content has been created and expert staff identified. Regardless of the type of RA content or services the library chooses to offer, it must be relevant to the library's service area. RA pages must be marketed well within the reading community and occupy a main position on the home page. Just as content is important, the technology used to publish it must be employed prudently. Technology should facilitate the end result: offering readers opportunities to learn about new authors and titles and the ability to share their experience with other readers.

RA WEB SITES TODAY

Qualities of exemplary RA web sites include visibility, clear purpose, logical organization, clean layout and loading speed, good content and links, relevance to the community, visual appeal, expertise and support, and promotion (Nordmeyer 2001). Many of these features can be applied to all types of web sites. Libraries can employ these basic principles of good web design in addition to the following suggestions for a successful RA page:

1. The RA page should be accessible from the main navigation bar so that readers can find it no matter what page they enter from.
2. The RA page should be clearly labeled so that nonlibrary users and library users can quickly identify where the link would lead.
3. RA pages for youth and adults should have appropriate designs that speak to their intended audience.

LEISURE READING IN ACADEMIC LIBRARIES

Although the mission of academic libraries is to support the course curriculum, some academic libraries provide a leisure reading collection for students and faculty. Academic libraries may find reasons to offer a leisure reading collection, including the distance to the local public library and their ability to serve students without further strain on public library staff and collections. "Browsing rooms are vestiges of the 1920's and 1930's, developed in an era when academic libraries vigorously promoted recreational reading interests of students" (Zauha 1993, 57). However, because of financial constraints and shifting resource allocation to the academic basis of curriculum support, many college and university libraries may not offer browsing collections for leisure reading. In the absence of a browsing collection, academic libraries may support leisure reading by creating a web page that provides external links to the public library or other web resources (Vesper).

Examples

The Browsing Room
  James E. Walker Library, Middle Tennessee State University
  http://www.mtsu.edu/~vvesper/brow.html
Recent additions to Savage Library's Popular Book Collection
  Leslie J. Savage Library, Western State College of Colorado
  http://www.western.edu/lib/info/rentals.html

VISIBILITY OF RA

One of the major difficulties encountered in a survey of public library web sites is the visibility of RA pages on the library's web site. Some libraries, such as the Public Library of Charlotte and Mecklenburg County (N.C.) (PLCMC), maintain web sites with identities entirely different from their libraries' web sites. PLCMC maintains both BookHive (*see* figure 7.1) (http://www. bookhive.org) and the Reader's Club (http://www.readersclub.org), for example.

Most libraries offer RA services off of their main page; however, many public library web sites fail to adequately label their RA services so readers can find them. An example of the variety of labels and some of the more common ones that libraries use to guide their readers to RA web pages follow:

> *The Reading Room,* Cleveland Public Library, http://www.cpl.org
>
> *Good Reads,* King County (Wash.) Public Library, http://www.kcls.org
>
> *Great Reads,* Columbus (Ohio) Metropolitan Library, http://www.cml.lib.oh.us
>
> *Recommended Reading,* Seattle Public Library, http://www.spl.org
>
> *Suggested Reading,* Brooklyn Public Library, http://www.brooklyn publiclibrary.org

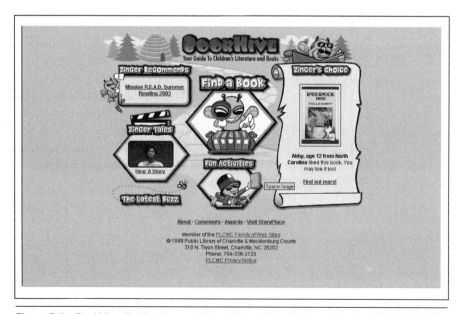

Figure 7.1   BookHive, Public Library of Charlotte and Mecklenburg County (N.C.). PLCMC's BookHive is a guide to children's literature and books.

LINKS TO EXTERNAL SITES

Many external sites exist that offer RA services, and readers expect libraries to offer well-organized links to these sites. These sites are sponsored by other libraries, publishers, authors, and organizations that promote reading. Among some of the popular categories are links to reading lists of best-sellers, book publishers and bookstores, book discussion guides, organizations sponsoring literary awards, links to e-books, links to literary magazines, and online book discussion groups. Libraries should not only link to these sites, but also study them and determine what appeal they have. Are they easy to navigate, professionally designed, rich with content? Adapt some of the better qualities to the library's web site.

Some of the most common RA links offered by libraries follow:

Book Spot
>   (http://www.bookspot.com)
>
>   Offers a great deal of content on categories such as best-sellers, book awards, reviews, online books, first chapters, genre fiction, online bookstores, authors, and publishers

Oprah Winfrey
>   (http://www.oprah.com; select Oprah's Books)
>
>   Lists all books selected by Oprah back to 1999 along with information about and from the authors, discussion boards, and readers' reactions to the books

The Book Report Network
>   (http://www.bookreporter.com)
>
>   Includes web sites that offer reading lists, support book discussion groups, and provide author interviews. These web sites appear to be supported, in part, by visitors' purchases of books from Amazon.com:
>
>>   http://www.readinggroupguides.com
>>
>>   http://www.bookreporter.com
>>
>>   http://www.teenreads.com
>>
>>   http://www.kidsreads.com
>>
>>   http://www.authorsontheweb.com

READING LISTS

Reading lists assist library customers in locating relevant material by creating thematic connections to books and by supplying readers with lists of favorite genres and authors (Kelly 2000). Libraries have traditionally provided their patrons with lists of reading materials in the form of bookmarks and bibliographies. Lists can be categorized by

> genre fiction
>
> reading level
>
> subject (nonfiction)
>
> forthcoming titles
>
> staff and patron recommendations
>
> age or grade level or both

Because most libraries are already creating lists in print, the content is already established; however, managing these lists becomes a challenge. If the library's ILS does not provide the functionality of retrieving lists from the bibliographic databases, then the library should explore ways to automate the publishing and posting of reading lists. Libraries can supplement lists with annotations, extracts, and reviews.

Libraries should establish the following guidelines:

Length. Length of the list should be no longer than two print pages unless a menu allows users to navigate the page easily.

Hypertext Links. Intuitively, users will want to click on the title for more information or to request it be sent to them. If your ILS allows it, all titles should be in italics and generate a link to the catalog.

Bibliographic Information. Depending on the genre, determine what elements of the bibliographic record are important to visitors. For a list, include call number or location, author, and title.

Frequency. Determine if the list should be published monthly, quarterly, or annually and whether to archive it.

Format. Format the list on the web page and provide a printer-friendly alternative. Patrons and staff may want to print the page without heavy graphics so they can make notes on it.

Examples

Coming Soon to a Shelf Near You
> Good Books, Las Vegas–Clark County Library District
> http://www.lvccld.org/good_books/coming_titles/index.cfm

New Materials List
> Webrary, Readers Services, Morton Grove (Ill.) Public Library
> http://www.webrary.org/rs/newnf.html

SUBSCRIPTION DATABASES

Libraries can also offer links to subscription-based online web sites that can aid visitors in discovering new authors and titles by reading reviews and author biographies. When libraries offer remote access to these online tools, visitors can access them anytime, anywhere, by simply typing in their library card number. The vendors of these products are also finding ways for users to link back to the library catalog during the user's session.

Books in Print (Bowker, 888-BOWKER2)
http://www.booksinprint.com

Books in Print (BIP) offers lists of best-sellers, brief author biographies, annotations, a section for children's literature, fiction, and forthcoming books. This electronic product also includes access to Bowker's database of more than 165,000 publishers, distributors, wholesalers, and book agents. *BIP* also allows users to check whether the library has a particular title by linking to the library catalog from the title information page. This product has a great deal of functionality and content that readers will enjoy; however, some of the screens, such as those offering ordering, are written for collection development staff. Also available: *Spanish Books in Print*.

NoveList (EBSCO, 800-758-5995)
http://www.epnet.com/public/novelist.asp

NoveList includes more than 100,000 titles in the database, 75,000 full-text reviews, and more than 36,000 subject headings. Users will be familiar with the product's "Find a Favorite Author" or "Find a Favorite Title" buttons. In addition, *NoveList* offers a great deal of content for staff training and support for RA services. Librarians and readers will also find book lists and book discussion guides to help support book discussion leaders.

What Do I Read Next? (Gale, 800-877-GALE)
http://www.galegroup.com

What Do I Read Next? includes more than 100,000 highly recommended adult, young adult, and children's fiction titles. The following print titles are also included in this database: *What Do I Read Next? What Do Young Adults Read Next? What Do Children Read Next? What Historical Novel Do I Read Next?* and *What Inspirational Literature Do I Read Next?*

BOOK REVIEWS

Book reviews often allow readers to determine whether they want to read a new book, especially those written by new or unknown authors. Additionally, subject specialists would benefit from reviews of new books in their field. The review serves not only as an informational tool, but as a marketing tool as well. Most RA services in public libraries are well established, and reviews are either already being written by staff or they are purchased for inclusion into the catalog. In some instances, libraries have created web sites based on reviews. Book reviews offer a constant stream of content for the library web site.

Staff Book Reviews

Because library staff members are typically avid readers, having them write reviews is well within their purview and adds great, homegrown content to a library web site. Libraries that purchase catalog-enriched content may also include reviews; however, allowing staff to create and post content offers a personalized touch that patrons appreciate and also offers staff an opportunity to contribute where they really excel.

Reader Book Reviews

A part of reading that is often overlooked is the opportunity to share the reader experience. Allowing readers to write reviews not only gives them the opportunity to express their thoughts, but it also allows them to participate in creating content for their library web site. The opportunity to submit content can create a feeling of ownership and help to produce a sticky web site with the hopes that reviewers will return frequently to see their reviews and read others.

Example

Reader's Club, Public Library of Charlotte and Mecklenburg County (N.C.)
    http://www.readersclub.org

> The Reader's Club allows visitors to read other customer reviews and input their own reviews for display on the web page.

AUTHORS ONLINE: E-MAIL AND REAL-TIME CHATS

Libraries that host author visits may want to consider various ways to promote author titles or upcoming author visits. Chats with an author can be interactive or recorded through e-mail as described below. However, libraries can also document an author's visit to the library by taking photographs, making video recordings, or transcribing the discussion in text or audio.

E-mail Chat

E-mail chat happens asynchronously when the library collects questions from its readers, forwards the questions on to an author, and posts the responses. Readers can submit their questions through an electronic form on the web site or on a paper form found at the public service desk. Questions are collected at the end of the submission period, organized, edited for review, and sent off to the author. The author is given a deadline by which to respond and e-mails his or her responses back to the library. The library then posts the questions and answers and often augments this with links to the catalog and the author's work, book jackets, reviews, and biographical information. Libraries can offer creative ways to access this material in addition to archiving it on their web site. The web page can be cataloged so that users searching the catalog will retrieve the web page if they search for the author.

Real-Time Chat

If an author agrees to a live chat, libraries must determine what chat service they will use, include directions for patrons to download necessary plug-ins, and publicize the event. Librarians can use the transcript to archive the exchange on the web site after the chat has ended. Live chat sessions involving multiple patrons should be moderated. Because it is difficult to predict a patron's behavior, libraries that offer this service may want to do it through a system that requires a library card because anonymity may entice a user to engage in improper conduct. The possibility of low turnout and participation may also plague an author visit set for a specific date and time. E-mail chat, although it does not sound as innovative and exciting as live chat, may be preferable for these very reasons.

RESPONDING TO READERS

The web site provides the perfect forum for interacting with visitors. In response to RA needs, two popular services librarians offer are patron suggestions for book purchases and custom bibliographies. Although these services may be quite staff-intensive, readers appreciate the personal touch they offer. After all, libraries serve their customers through responsive collections, and who would be better to suggest titles for reading lists but a librarian!

Suggest a Book

If readers find that the library has not acquired an item they would like to borrow, they may appreciate the opportunity to submit their suggestions. Depending on whether a library has centralized collection development tasks, staff can submit their suggestions, too. Although valuable for reader input, this is clearly a staff-intensive request. Some suggestions submitted by patrons may be more suitable as an interlibrary loan request. Many patrons also want a follow-up response on whether the library is going to purchase the material. Appropriate statements should be posted with the form so that viewers can be redirected to the ILL submission form, the library's collection development policy, or a statement that indicates follow-up procedures.

Examples

Duke University Libraries (N.C.)
    http://www.lib.duke.edu/colldev/ask4book.htm
George C. Gordon Library, Worcester (Mass.) Polytechnic Institute
    http://www.wpi.edu/Academics/Library/Services/suggestpurchase.html
Harris County (Tex.) Public Library
    http://www.hcpl.lib.tx.us/br/bookreq.htm

Customized Bibliographies

Another popular service is a user-requested bibliography. This is similar to a reference query in that it provides individualized service and is patron-initiated. Patrons can fill out a form on the library web site requesting a reading list be sent to them via e-mail, fax, or mail. Although this is a service that is typically provided to patrons without special forms, many users and nonusers still do not understand the services that libraries provide. A form on the Web gives visitors the opportunity to ask for help in a very neutral place.

BOOK DISCUSSION GROUPS

Library-Sponsored Book Discussion Groups

Web sites offer great publicity for book discussion groups. Information about a branch's book discussion group should be displayed on the events listing as well as in the information about the library. Include a listing of titles so readers can do their reading before attending the first meeting. Questions about the book can also be posted so readers have time for reflection prior to the book discussion. You can also use this page to send to the local bookstores or other appropriate places to market the group's activities.

Online Book Discussion Groups

Libraries may choose to offer their own online book discussion groups. Some of the challenges of online discussion include scheduling. The convenience of the Internet diminishes when you have a certain time you must attend your discussion group. Many discussion groups favor using a bulletin board. That way, readers can come and go as they please, reading and posting at their leisure. Just as in a physical meeting, a library staff member normally leads the group as moderator. Schedules for titles are created, and comments are accepted either indefinitely or they cease on a certain date. The discussion is normally archived for all viewers to read.

Other libraries work with e-mail list managers so that the discussion is posted via e-mail. Libraries can choose to test out some of the bulletin board messaging systems, such as Yahoo! groups (http://groups.yahoo.com), before they decide on which is best for them.

Many resources are available from publishers to help librarians prepare reading guides for book discussions. Publishers such as HarperCollins (http://www.harpercollins.com/hc/readers), Simon & Schuster (http://www.simonsays.com), and Ballantine (http://www.randomhouse.com/BRC/) offer reading guides. Reading guides include author biographies, chapter excerpts, plot summaries, topics for discussion, and information on starting a reading group.

Supporting Readers' Book Discussions

Libraries are learning to market their materials in new ways by taking multiple copies of previous best-sellers appropriate for book discussions and packaging them as kits. Libraries provide eight to ten or more copies of the same title, include information about the book and possible discussion avenues, and offer them to local groups.

Examples

Kenton County (Ky.) Public Library
   http://www.kenton.lib.ky.us/information/kits/index.html

Las Vegas–Clark County Library District
   http://www.lvccld.org/good_books/discussion_kits/index.cfm

RA WEB SITES TOMORROW

Although RA is a cornerstone of library business, its development on library web sites remains in its infancy. As the library catalog evolves into a more reader-centered tool, RA will continue to develop into the potential as a driving force to circulate the library's collection. In addition, as library RA sites become more interactive, an "open, online dialogue and sharing of interpretations between people lend a deeper meaning to fiction itself" (Kelly 2000, 24). "The next step must be entering the live environment to negotiate and guide the public as well as to personalize services" (Feldman and Strobel 2002). The sharing of readers' thoughts and interpretations of what they read is the focal point of RA. With this interaction, technology will actually allow RA to flourish rather than impede its progress.

For more information

Adult Reading Round
> http://www.arrtreads.org
>
> Founded in 1984 to promote reader's advisory service and fiction collections in public and school libraries in Illinois.

Center for the Book in the Library of Congress
> http://www.loc.gov/loc/cfbook
>
> Established in 1977. Works closely with other organizations to foster understanding of the vital role of books, reading, libraries, and literacy in society. Links to state center affiliates.

Fiction-L
> http://www.webrary.org/rs/flmenu.html
>
> An electronic mailing list devoted to RA topics developed for and by librarians.

Reader's Advisory Sources, RUSA, ALA
> http://www.ala.org/rusa/bestbooks.html
>
> RUSA (ALA) links to Best Books and other award-winning lists of books.

Teen Reading
> http://www.ala.org/teenread
>
> Resources for libraries offering RA services for teens. Includes reading lists and information on Teen Read Week.

EIGHT

Content for Specific Audiences

Libraries have typically reached out to certain segments of the population by creating programs and identifying collections that are relevant to their needs. In addition to offering relevant content, the creation of web pages for specific audiences aids in improved design and navigation. "Audience-oriented schemes break a site into smaller, audience-specific mini-sites, thereby allowing for clutter-free pages which present only the options of interest to that particular audience" (Rosenfeld and Morville 2002, 61).

To create web content that appeals to specific audiences, it is important to understand their information-seeking behaviors and the type of online activities in which they engage. *A Nation Online: How Americans Are Expanding Their Use of the Internet* concluded that gender, age, race, and income have some relationship with Internet users' selection of online activities (U.S. National Telecommunications and Information Administration 2002). In addition to online behavior of users, libraries should review local demographic data to determine groups most represented in their service area. General studies and surveys should be used in conjunction with local data and input when planning on creating content that will engage a library's service area most.

As in any programming efforts, it is important to seek input from the target audience during the planning phases of development. Members of the group will be best able to identify images and terminology considered stereotypical or inappropriate for the target audience. Including group members in the planning stages, seeking their input, and implementing some of their ideas may aid in greater acceptance by the intended audience. The greater the involvement of the target audience in the development of the web site, the better the chances are for its success. Libraries should follow these eight steps:

1. Identify a focus group within the target audience. Focus group members can come from local organizations and both users and nonusers of the library.
2. Generate ideas for content. Provide the focus group with a list of content and ask them to prioritize in order of relevancy. Give the group an opportunity to list additional content and services not currently offered by the library.
3. Review the prioritized list. Discuss content sources with public service and special programming staff and graphics with the web designer.
4. Develop a time line. Take into consideration the amount of time that it may take to develop web pages that need special programming. Decide whether the project should be divided into two phases.
5. The web designer creates a prototype. A prototype may not include all of the functionality; however, it allows for a visual representation demonstrating the navigation and structure of the documents.
6. Web pages are posted for beta testing. The focus group provides evaluation and feedback during this stage.
7. Web pages are posted to the public.
8. Market the site. Ask members of the focus group to aid in advertising the web site to its community.

Studies and surveys help libraries determine what motivates certain people to go online and, more specifically, to the library web site. Libraries should ask themselves these questions:

What are specific needs of this group and what motivates them to go online?

How can those needs be met by the library web site?

How do we best present the information?

Libraries typically choose to create specialized web pages for the following groups:

Academic Libraries	*Public Libraries*
Alumni	Business professionals
Undergraduate students	Children
Graduate students	New residents
Faculty	Non-English speakers
Distance education students	Parents
International students	Seniors
Reentry students	Teachers
Students with disabilities	Teenagers

DIVERSIFYING YOUR WEB SITE

Librarians determine the demographic makeup of their patrons by seeing who comes through the door each day and by reviewing local statistical documents to learn about nonusers, or the community in general. Monthly web statistics gleaned from log analysis software retrieve aggregate data about information such as the type of Internet browser the visitors use, operating system, and amount of time spent on the site. However, the software, or course, cannot report on the age, religion, gender, race, or religion of the visitors. It would be impossible to identify the social characteristics of users unless a survey was taken. Libraries who have infused diversity into their staff, collections, and programs can also incorporate diversity into their web sites. Libraries may find that by using a variety of images depicting staff, patrons, and students from all ages and races, visitors may feel more receptive when they see images of staff or people that resemble them either in race or age. But images alone are merely a beginning.

Many libraries have formed diversity committees to address issues affecting their libraries. Some of these focus on the hiring and retention of a diverse workforce. Many libraries strive to create a workforce that mirrors its community. It is important to publish the library's diversity initiatives on the employment page, including a link to the library's diversity policy, or link to information on ways in which the library addresses the diversity within its community.

Programs and Events

Libraries offer a rich amount of cultural programs such as film festivals, art exhibits, dance, bilingual story times, and English classes. The web site can serve not only as a means of advertising for these events, but it can also be used to offer supplementary material. For example, libraries that celebrate Asian

Pacific, Hispanic, African American, and Native American Heritage Months can include content such as images, reading lists, related web sites, and kids' coloring pages (*see* figure 8.1). These materials can remain on the web site year-round by simply removing the events information after the events are over.

More Ideas for Promoting Diversity on the Web Site

To promote diversity on your web site, try the following:

> Include a statement about diversity within your electronic resources collection development plan and make sure the collection mirrors the needs of your community.

> Include links to local organizations that support various segments of the community.

> Include appropriate images on pages for specific audiences. For example, include seniors on the seniors' page, teens on the teens' page, and kids on the kids' page—of all races.

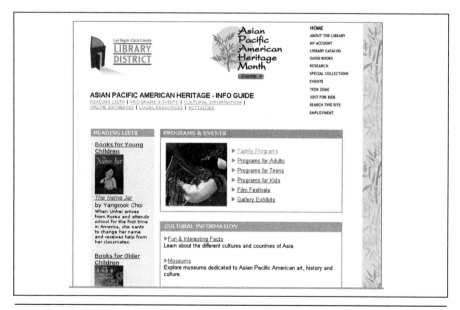

Figure 8.1 Asian Pacific American Heritage Month, Las Vegas–Clark County (Nev.) Library. The Las Vegas–Clark County Library District celebrates Asian Pacific American Heritage Month with programs, reading lists, cultural information, and access to relevant online databases and local resources.

Include links to newspapers from various countries representative of ethnic origins of students or community residents.

For more information
Office for Diversity, ALA
http://www.ala.org; select Our Association, Offices, Diversity

YOUNG PEOPLE

Children's services in libraries have long been equated with reading, good books, and story times. Once preschoolers become school-aged children and young adults, they also use the library to assist them in finding materials for their homework. Using the Web to deliver the information to them is an appropriate method because most students are proficient in computer and Internet use. When libraries understand the online habits of young adults, they will be better prepared to serve them online. Recent studies indicate that children and young adults also use the Internet for communications and entertainment. Children or young adults are more likely to use the Internet to complete school assignments or play games; e-mail is a close second to schoolwork among teenagers and young adults. Participating in chat rooms, listening to radio stations, and watching television and movies are among the top online activities that these two age groups engage in (U.S. National Telecommunications and Information Administration 2002).

The Children's Online Privacy Protection Act of 1998 (COPPA) requires commercial online content providers to obtain parental consent if they seek out personal information from a child age twelve or younger. If age requirements are not listed online, companies must still comply with this law if their content is geared for children that age (ALA 2003). Although libraries are exempt from COPPA, they should provide a link to their privacy statement when collecting personally identifiable information through the web site, for example, if children are asked to fill out an online form to sign up for the summer reading program or perhaps enter a contest.

Libraries offer homework help to students by creating web pages with relevant online databases, real-time reference, live tutors, and a kid's version of the library catalog. The Broward County (Fla.) Library offers a kid's catalog (*see* figure 8.2) that limits its holdings to materials classified as juvenile literature. Design for children normally includes large and colorful graphics, sparse text, bigger fonts, and easy search screens.

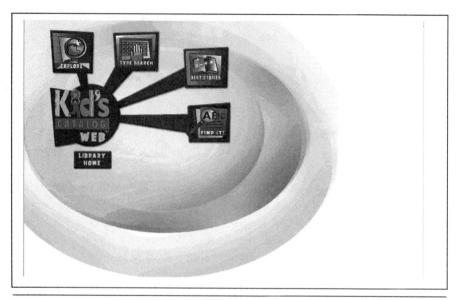

Figure 8.2   Kid's Catalog at the Broward County (Fla.) Library

In addition, libraries can offer young people bibliographies on frequently requested topics such as

biographies	geography
presidents	educational games
scientists	careers
inventions and inventors	almanacs
North American Indian tribes	rain forests
history and time lines	mythology
pets	English: poems, monologues, riddles, and jokes
science projects and experiments	finding images
plants and animals	
places: cities, states, countries	

A noteworthy library web site, StoryPlace, created by the Public Library of Charlotte and Mecklenburg County (N.C.) and the recipient of numerous awards, provides content for preschool- and elementary-age children, including themes such as dinosaurs, crocodiles, animals, and trains (*see* figure 8.3). Each theme offers online activities, crafts, and reading lists. BookHive, a sister site, provides guides to literature and books for this age group.

Figure 8.3 StoryPlace, Public Library of Charlotte and Mecklenburg County (N.C.). Created by the Public Library of Charlotte and Mecklenburg County, StoryPlace (http://www.storyplace.org) offers content for preschool- and elementary-age children.

Teens

In addition to school-related uses of the Internet, teenagers go online for a variety of other activities, including to communicate with friends and family via e-mail and chat; to entertain themselves by going to web sites about movies, TV shows, music groups, or sports stars; to find information on hobbies and news; to get insight into what's cool; to make online purchases and do comparative shopping (among older teens); to play or download online games; to learn things largely unrelated to school; to explore other online interactive transactions; to visit chat rooms; to visit web pages for clubs, groups, or sports teams to which they belong; to trade or sell things; or to look for fitness, dieting, or health information (mostly older girls) (Lenhart, Rainie, and Lewis 2001).

Teens are also looking for ways to express themselves and either visit sites where they can express their opinion about something or create their own web sites (Lenhart, Rainie, and Lewis 2001). TeensPoint.org, a creation of the Central Rappahannock Regional Library (Va.), is a database-driven web site that invites teen input in areas like books, movies, music, web sites, and short stories (*see* figure 8.4). TeensPoint.org also features an ongoing poetry slam.

Figure 8.4 TeensPoint.org, Central Rappahannock (Va.) Regional Library. TeensPoint.org (http://www.teenspoint.org/reviews/web.asp) posts teen-authored web reviews. Entries include screen shots, and reviewers assign one to five stars to each site.

The ability for teens to publish their own words on the library's web site is highly appealing, and the constantly changing content motivates them to return to the site frequently. Not only does TeensPoint.org offer teens the opportunity to express themselves, but the web page is also tied to a program offered in the branch. Teens who write web reviews for the site meet monthly to socialize and share their opinions. Teens review web sites based on usability and the informational, recreational, and grade-level interest (Purdy 2002). Successful library teen web sites will often include a tie to a program offered in the branches, which may generate content for the Web, or the Web will be used to publish supplementary material for the program. This way, the web site promotes programming, while the program drives visitors back to the site.

In *Teens.Library*, Braun reviews how teen developmental needs are met by use of the Web. Categories outlined by the Search Institute's Developmental Assets for Adolescents include support, empowerment, boundaries and expectations, constructive use of time, commitment to learning, positive values, social competencies, and positive identity (Braun 2002). Ideas for creating content for teens follow:

Career and job information

College preparation

Consumer information

Fashion

Hobbies

Poetry

Polls

Reviews: music, movies, television shows, books, web sites

School sports

For more information

Virtual YA Index

http://yahelp.suffolk.lib.ny.us/virtual.html

Lists public libraries with young adult web pages.

SENIORS

Seniors make up a majority of the public library user base, and universities are serving an increasing number of older, or returning, students. *Library Services to Older Adults Guidelines* should be consulted when creating online content and services for seniors (ALA 1999). People age fifty-five and older were more likely than any other age group to check health information online, and those age fifty-five and older showed equally strong e-mail use as any other adult age group (U.S. National Telecommunications and Information Administration 2002). In addition to creating content for the senior population, the Web can also be used to publish information that may supplement a program offered to this user group. For example, web pages promoting computer workshops can include information about the class content. Seniors can then print the materials in preparation for the class.

As mentioned previously, learning about the type of activities the targeted audience performs online can help libraries that want to use their web sites to reach this group. A survey of 2,084 adults age fifty and older showed the top five things that seniors do online: (1) stay in touch with friends and relatives, (2) stay current with news and events, (3) research health information, (4) make purchases online, and (5) research various other topics. Additionally, this user group surfs the Internet to find consumer information such as computer software or hardware options; travel packages, plane tickets, and rental cars; books; automobiles; and other electronics (SeniorNet 2002).

Making Your Web Site Senior Friendly offers the following suggestions for the presentation of text and page design (U.S. National Library of Medicine 2001):

> *Typeface*: Use a sans serif typeface like Helvetica, Arial, Universe or News Gothic.
>
> *Type Size*: Use 12 or 14 point for body text.
>
> *Type Weight*: Use medium or bold face type.
>
> *Layout*: Use capital and lowercase letters, double-space all body text, and left justify text.
>
> *Color*: Avoid yellow and blue and green in close proximity with use of graphics and text that are difficult for some older adults to discriminate.
>
> *Backgrounds*: Use dark type or graphics against a light background, or use white lettering on a dark background. Avoid patterned backgrounds.

LANGUAGE-RELATED GROUPS

Libraries are increasingly serving a multilingual population. After English, the five most commonly spoken languages at home for people over the age of five in the United States are Spanish, Chinese, French, German, and Tagalog (U.S. Bureau of the Census 2000b). Libraries purchase materials in non-English languages depending on their customer base or curriculum they support. Integrated library systems now offer interfaces in languages other than English, and services such as real-time reference and live tutors that are offered in Spanish have entered the library market.

International students, depending on their country of origin, may benefit from an in-depth tutorial that outlines services provided by the library. International students, who may not be accustomed to library services, may require more instruction than other students. They may also learn best in their native language. A web-based tutorial allows them to learn at their own pace. The William and Anita Newman Library at Baruch College (N.Y.) offers a tour available in nine languages in both HTML and Macromedia Flash as illustrated in figure 8.5. The web design, animation, audio file creation, and image processing were accomplished using standard web development tools such as Photoshop, Illustrator, Flash, Dreamweaver, Premier, and Peak LP (Downing

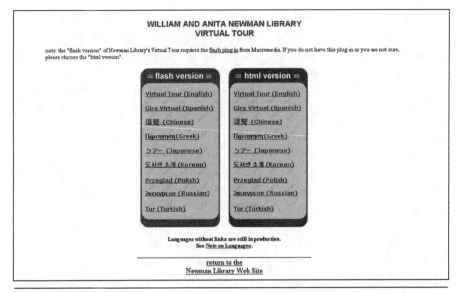

Figure 8.5 The William and Anita Newman Library Virtual Tour, Baruch College (N.Y.). The William and Anita Newman Library offers a library tour available in nine languages: English, Spanish, Chinese, Greek, Japanese, Korean, Polish, Russian, and Turkish. It is available at http://newman.baruch.cuny.edu/about/v_tour/.

and Klein 2001). The library relies on volunteers of native speakers of target languages who are also fluent in English.

A variety of techniques are used to publish nonroman alphabets on the Web. Browsers must also be able to display the code. When trying to access a web page using nonroman scripts, viewers may be prompted to download language extensions from their browsers. Operating systems must also have language support. Additionally, language-specific pages must use country- or culture-specific displays (or both), such as colors, symbols, and graphics, appropriately (Bayan 2001). Equally important to creating content for non-English languages is the ability for third-party applications to manage it, including databases, content management scripts, systems, servers, and e-commerce tools. All systems must have the capability to support the special character sets of non-English languages.

Spanish-Language Library Web Sites

The user population that has the greatest numbers for most libraries is the Spanish-speaking community. Many libraries have not only created web sites in Spanish, but have also implemented a Spanish-language catalog for this user population. Language is not the sole identifying factor when providing such services, and providing services to this group can prove to be complex because issues involve not only language, but also nationality, regional, and cultural differences. The *Guidelines for Library Services to Hispanics* notes that there are significant linguistic and cultural differences reflected in the varieties of Spanish spoken by Mexicans, Puerto Ricans, Cubans, and other Hispanic groups (ALA 1988). This guiding document offers libraries a baseline from which to work when creating services for this group. In addition, libraries should tap the resources of REFORMA, an organization that promotes the development of Spanish-language and Latino-oriented library collections; the recruitment of bilingual, multicultural library personnel; and public awareness of libraries and librarianship among Latinos.

Typically, library web sites for Spanish speakers include the following information: library services (location, contact information, hours of operation, how to obtain a library card); collections (Spanish-language catalog, links to databases and sites in Spanish); and information about events (bilingual story time and classes or programs in Spanish). Several libraries offer exemplary Spanish-language web sites, such as the Phoenix (Ariz.) Public Library (*see* figure 8.6).

Libraries that offer a Spanish-language catalog will find that, although their library catalog vendor offers a plain vanilla catalog "out of the box," they will still spend a great deal of time revising it so that it will mirror any customization and features included in the English catalog. Additionally, librarians may find that if the language is not entirely appropriate for their community and it must be slightly modified, this may include many hours of customization. Furthermore, any functionality must be reflected in the catalog's help files.

Libraries that offer a Spanish-language catalog typically do so because a substantial portion of their collection is in Spanish. Unfortunately, many librarians fail to realize that unless the MARC records for the materials include Spanish-language subject headings, although the catalog is in Spanish, the items remain accessible only through a keyword search. The catalog is a shell that merely supplies a user interface and search mechanism for the collection.

Creider notes that the increase in the Hispanic population has been accompanied by an increase in the number of catalog records in OCLC with topical subject headings in Spanish. Creider conducted a survey of the libraries of Hispanic-serving institutions and associate members of the Hispanic Association of Colleges and Universities to determine how the headings were being used in local catalogs. The survey indicated that, although few academic libraries assign such headings locally, many retain and display them in the catalog when they are provided through copy cataloging records (Creider 2003).

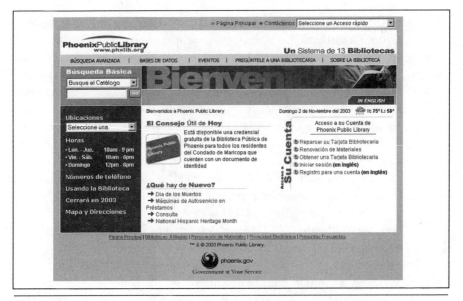

Figure 8.6   Biblioteca Publica de Phoenix, Phoenix (Ariz.) Public Library. The Phoenix Public Library offers a wide range of web content for Spanish-speaking visitors (http://www.phoenixpubliclibrary.org/spanish/index.jsp).

For more information

Bibliotecas Para la Gente, Northern California Chapter of REFORMA
   http://www.bibliotecasparalagente.org/sujetos.html

   Offers resources for libraries serving Spanish speakers, including a link to Spanish-language subject headings provided by the Oakland and San Francisco (Calif.) Public Libraries.

REFORMA
   http://www.reforma.org

   National organization to promote library and information services to Latinos and the Spanish-speaking community.

ACCESSIBILITY: SERVICES TO PEOPLE WITH DISABILITIES

The Web has touched virtually every aspect of society and in many cases has replaced traditional sources of information. An audience well served by accessible library content and services via the Web is people with disabilities. This includes people who are blind and visually impaired and those who have hearing, speech, physical, cognitive, and neurological disabilities. According to the U.S. Bureau of the Census, 19.3 percent of the people over the age of five suffer from some type of disability (2000a). People with disabilities now have the option to purchase many items online, including groceries, so long as the web page is authored in a way that assistive technology can read, access, and complete e-commerce transactions. Accessing information online allows this group of users to maintain their independence without the assistance of an intermediary to find and deliver the information. It also protects their privacy, because people they interact with online may not know of their disability. With the library's mission to provide equitable access to all constituents—coupled with the knowledge that accessible pages make good sense—libraries would be irresponsible *not* to create accessible web sites.

Without special treatment of the web site, people with disabilities may not be able to access certain web content. To experience a glimpse of what a disabled person views on a web site, turn off the images in the browser and use the tab key to navigate through the links displayed on the page. If images are not identified by descriptors (ALT text tag), it is difficult to decipher the context of the graphics, especially when many navigation bars are created with graphics. Valenza discusses a disabled user's experience (2000, 35):

> Because screen readers move horizontally across a page, columns, tables, and frames scrambled the text and made it unintelligible. And Kelly couldn't see the images she missed. She couldn't see visually presented searching cues, the clickable buttons, the search boxes, and other graphic commands. She couldn't tell where one result ended and another began.

The two most frequently performed tasks by people with disabilities include using the Internet to send and receive electronic mail and searching for information (Kaye 2000). More facts from Kaye's report regarding online behavior follow:

Thirty-nine percent of Internet users with disabilities read the news online, check the weather forecast, or obtain sports scores.

Almost 30 percent take courses over the Internet or use online resources to help with schoolwork.

One-quarter of Internet users with disabilities use the Internet for job-related tasks, a significantly lower figure than the 43.1 percent of Internet users without disabilities, who are more likely to have jobs.

One-sixth (17.0 percent) use the Internet for shopping, paying bills, or other commercial activities.

Almost 16 percent use it to look for employment opportunities.

One of the underlying practices that web developers should employ is always offering alternative access to materials. For example, in addition to the navigation bar made from images, text links representing the main navigation bar should appear at the bottom of the page. Also, creating a page titled Accessibility available from the home page can offer a description of usability techniques used throughout the web site, catalog, and online databases, informing visitors what materials have been made accessible.

As you will see from the guidelines listed below, accessibility goes far beyond ALT tags used to identify images on web pages. Efforts such as the Web Accessibility Initiative (WAI), sponsored by the World Wide Web Consortium (W3C) and the HTML Writers Guild's AWARE (Accessible Web Authoring Resources and Education Center), assist web site developers in creating usable and accessible sites for people with disabilities. The W3C, through its WAI, has created *Web Content Accessibility Guidelines 1.0* (also defined as checkpoints), which include the following fourteen guidelines (W3C 1999):

1. Provide equivalent alternatives to auditory and visual content.
2. Don't rely on color alone.
3. Use markup and style sheets properly.
4. Clarify natural language usage.
5. Create tables that transform gracefully.
6. Ensure that pages featuring new technologies transform gracefully.
7. Ensure user control of time-sensitive content changes.
8. Ensure direct accessibility of embedded user interfaces.
9. Design for device independence.
10. Use interim solutions.
11. Use W3C technologies and guidelines.
12. Provide context and orientation information.
13. Provide clear navigation mechanisms.
14. Ensure that documents are clear and simple.

In addition, there is government legislation that addresses the provision of accessibility, such as Americans with Disabilities Act (ADA) and Public Law 102-569, Section 508. Standards apply to federal web sites but not to private sector web sites, unless a site is provided under contract to a federal agency, in which case only that web site or the portion covered by the contract would have to comply (U.S. 1998 Amendment to Section 508 of the Rehabilitation Act 1998). Many web sites check their pages for Section 508 and WAI compliancy. Noncompliance with current accessibility standards blocks access to materials and services to a large group of users.

WAI organizes accessibility requirements according to three priority levels. Priority one includes requirements that web designers must satisfy for basic accessibility, such as text equivalent for every nontext element, information available without color, and identifying row and column headers. Priority two lists requirements that web designers should complete or one or more groups will find it difficult to access the material, such as providing foreground and background color combinations that contrast and alternative pages if dynamic content is not accessible. Priority three lists guidelines designers may choose to follow for the greatest amount of accessibility, including creating logical tab order through links and forms on each page and providing keyboard shortcuts to important links (W3C 1999). Each priority addresses general requirements such as tables, frames, forms, applets, scripts, images, image maps, and multimedia files. Each priority is explained in detail, and associated techniques are offered to satisfy the requirement. Web developers who need to compare Section 508 compliancy with the W3C's checkpoints and priority levels can access this information at the Section 508 web site (http://www.section508.gov).

The following standards are requirements of Section 508:

§ 1194.22 Web-based intranet and Internet information and applications

A text equivalent for every nontext element shall be provided (e.g., via "alt," "longdesc," or in element content).

Equivalent alternatives for any multimedia presentation shall be synchronized with the presentation.

Web pages shall be designed so that all information conveyed with color is also available without color, for example, from context or markup.

Documents shall be organized so they are readable without requiring an associated style sheet.

Redundant text links shall be provided for each active region of a server-side image map.

Client-side image maps shall be provided instead of server-side image maps except where the regions cannot be defined with an available geometric shape.

Row and column headers shall be identified for data tables.

Markup shall be used to associate data cells and header cells for data tables that have two or more logical levels of row or column headers.

Frames shall be titled with text that facilitates frame identification and navigation.

Pages shall be designed to avoid causing the screen to flicker with a frequency greater than 2 Hz and lower than 55 Hz.

A text-only page, with equivalent information or functionality, shall be provided to make a web site comply with the provisions of this part, when compliance cannot be accomplished in any other way. The content of the text-only page shall be updated whenever the primary page changes.

When pages utilize scripting languages to display content, or to create interface elements, the information provided by the script shall be identified with functional text that can be read by assistive technology.

When a web page requires that an applet, plug-in, or other application be present on the client system to interpret page content, the page must provide a link to a plug-in or applet that complies with §1194.21(a) through (l). [Software Applications and Operating Systems]

When electronic forms are designed to be completed online, the form shall allow people using assistive technology to access the information, field elements, and functionality required for completion and submission of the form, including all directions and cues.

A method shall be provided that permits users to skip repetitive navigation links.

When a timed response is required, the user shall be alerted and given sufficient time to indicate that more time is required.

Accessibility to Third-Party Vendors

Libraries evaluate subscription databases, e-books, and electronic services for their ease of use, subject coverage, authority of the publisher, output options, and remote access, but it is difficult to determine if libraries have made accessibility a requirement for purchase. Some vendors have released ADA-compliant versions of their informational databases. Libraries must require vendors to create accessible versions of their products; otherwise, libraries will build accessible web pages leading to a path of inaccessible information. A study of the Technology Access Program (TAP) at Oregon State University found that "since the fall of 1999 when the last informal evaluation was completed by TAP we have seen almost a complete reversal in the inaccessibility of the online library databases from approximately 95% inaccessible to 95% accessible" (Stewart 2003).

Libraries can use the following four questions from the DO-IT (Disabilities, Opportunities, Internet-working, and Technology) web site as guidelines for assessing accessibility practices (University of Washington 2001):

1. Can the library's electronic and information resources, including web pages, online catalogs, indexes, and full-text databases and CD-ROMs, be accessed with a variety of adaptive computer technologies such as screen readers and speech synthesis?
2. Do library policy statements specifically state that electronic products should be evaluated for accessibility as part of the procurement process?
3. Do library web page development guidelines require that pages be designed in an accessible format?
4. Are librarians prepared to assist patrons with electronic resources that they cannot access by providing research consultations or materials in other formats?

Authoring content using the guidelines described above not only allows for greater accessibility for patrons with low or no vision, but some of these same authoring principles can be applied for content creation intended for PDAs, such as empty ALT tags, which represent images that act as placeholders in a web page (Kirkpatrick 2003). Populations such as the baby boomers, as well as the younger generations, who are already web dependent, will most likely require web content providers have an even greater commitment to accessibility (Valenza 2000). Librarians will continue to juggle the importance of including multimedia content such as streaming audio and video, which pose a challenge to screen readers and other assistive technologies, and providing equitable access to all visitors.

NINE

Library Web Sites: Where Do We Go from Here?

Library web sites have increased in complexity during the last several years, transforming from mere descriptions of services and collections to actually offering them online through the Web. Library web sites are multifaceted and backed by powerful, robust databases. Although there is still much work to be done, the library profession has progressed quickly in this area for several reasons. Much of the foundation for many of the services already existed. For example, guiding documents and standards, both from libraries and professional organizations, have already been created within reference, reader's advisory, and circulation services. Additionally, our noncompetitive marketplace allows us to share information freely about how we create web sites, the technology we use, and whether it was successful or not, and why. Librarians share information in a variety of ways, including electronic discussion groups, conferences, and library literature. This has allowed us to learn from one another's successes and failures.

Libraries share common goals that typically include the collection, organization, storage, and dissemination of information. Although the delivery method of information has evolved throughout the years, these basic similarities remain. Information has been recorded on clay tablets, bone, papyrus, paper, microfiche, microfilm, CD-ROMs, and, most recently, through the World Wide Web. Standards for publishing electronic books continue to evolve, and communication software has also been developed to help us do much of our business over the Internet. Library automation vendors have developed web-enabled catalogs so that libraries have a way to organize and make collections available to visitors twenty-four hours a day, seven days a week. Librarians have eagerly taken advantage of the Web to offer access to online collections and services.

Librarians have continued to adapt to new technology and find ways to improve services by making library services much more accessible. The Internet has threatened libraries (information is very accessible, everything is online, we don't need libraries) and, at the same time, has provided librarians with so many opportunities (access the library from home, chat with a librarian, full-text information on demand). In conclusion, several issues and trends have emerged that will impact library web site development.

ADMINISTRATIVE ISSUES

The privacy of patron information, security of web content, copyright, and digital rights management, together with budgetary and staffing issues, are concerns that need to be addressed at some point in the web site development process, preferably sooner than later. Furthermore, many libraries struggle with creating specific staffing models that work; however, the most successful ones are distributed. The library web site has implications for every part of the organization. Each person who works on the web site comes to the table with certain expertise: public service staff offer services, the technology department administers the server and may provide advanced programming skills, the web designer offers design and usability skills, technical services staff bring with them the knowledge of cataloging, collection development staff purchase content, and the public relations department puts a user-friendly face on it all. Maintaining a clearly articulated vision and understanding each department's responsibility is crucial in making this staffing model successful.

TECHNOLOGY

Technology concerns obviously have far-reaching implications, including creating a scalable web site based on the latest standards that will continue to be accessible from library terminals as well as by remote visitors. The web site, its scripts, and software must also behave with the web server. Additional concerns include authentication, statistical reporting, compatibility among third-party vendors, and, equally important, keeping it all running on a twenty-four-hour basis.

USER-CENTERED DESIGN

Creating a user-centered web site is quite often the topic of many articles in library literature. This is probably in reaction to first-generation web sites, which tended to mirror a library's organizational structure. Librarians are now routinely conducting usability testing of our web sites and sharing the results with others in the library profession. This testing tends to address the labels librarians use and the way in which we group collections and services on the web site. It is quite possible that what works on one web site will also work on another. Other user-centered initiatives include the creation of library portals, user-specific entry pages, and customization of the catalog. Reports like the *Use and Users of Electronic Library Resources: An Overview and Analysis of Recent Research Studies* (available at http://www.clir.org), which analyzes more than 200 recent research publications that focus on the use of electronic resources, assist us in learning the online behaviors of customers, thus creating more user-centered web sites for them. Reports like this will continue to assist libraries in understanding customer needs.

FULL-TEXT CONTENT

The increasing amount of full-text content available on library web sites and through the library catalog is staggering. As the number of databases rises, librarians find it is increasingly difficult for patrons to find the appropriate database to answer their questions. Many of the resources go unused. Enter resource integration software. Vendors promise a one-stop search interface for databases and the catalog. Additionally, OpenURL standards promise to link visitors from a database containing only a bibliographic citation to the database where the full text of the article appears. More full-text content is a boon for researchers; however, librarians need to keep up on access issues and copyright, ownership, and licensing.

THIRD-PARTY VENDORS

Many libraries that contract with such third-party vendors as aggregated databases, electronic books, and content enrichment suppliers for the catalog must manage those accounts accordingly. This includes troubleshooting technical problems, including downtime and access issues; managing contracts from the various vendors; licensing limits on simultaneous users; keeping current vendor contacts; and alerting staff and customers to product upgrades. Additionally, libraries must be knowledgeable about minimum browser requirements and plug-ins required to run the system as well as gathering monthly statistics for each product.

E-COMMERCE

Appearing as a bleep on the radar is the entrance of e-commerce into library web sites. Libraries are slowly engaging in commercial activity online. Many times this functionality is in place so that patrons can pay for fines, lost materials, printouts, office supplies, and used books. E-commerce calls for secure servers, relationships with bankers, and dependence on standards so that the integrated library system talks to the debit and credit card machines.

Libraries will continue to improve, upgrade, and revise their web sites, and as they find that an increasing amount of business is conducted online, libraries will move more and more resources in support of online collections and services. An increase in the amount of business conducted online and future technological advances will compel libraries to address many of the issues inherent to the delivery of online services so that staff and resources are in place to meet customer demand.

THE COMPANION WEB PAGES

The author is maintaining an online presence to supplement this book at http://www.webliography.org/ala. This companion web page contains an online version of the editorial calendar, examples of spreadsheets used to collect statistics, updated company information found in appendix B, and more information pertaining to virtual libraries.

APPENDIX A

Editorial Calendar

EDITORIAL CALENDAR DATES and DEADLINES 2003						Last Revised 2/18/03
Event	*Contact*	*Submit*	*Review Period*	*Post*	*Event Date*	*Web Page*
JANUARY						
New Year's Day	Libraries closed	11/20	12/5/02 through 12/10/02	12/15	1/1	Home page
Tax Season	Ref. committee	12/10	12/20/02 through 12/27/02	12/29	1/1 through 4/15	Research pages
Martin Luther King, Jr.'s Birthday	Libraries closed	1/2	1/2/03 through 1/6/03	1/7	1/20	Home page
FEBRUARY						
African American History Month	Lisa	12/7	1/7/03 through 1/13/03	1/15	February	Home page with rotating graphics
Book Lover's Month	John	1/15	1/25/03 through 1/29/03	2/1	February	Home page, reading corner
President's Day	Libraries closed	2/1	2/2/03 through 2/3/03	2/4	2/17	Home page
American Heart Month	Flo	1/15	1/20/03 through 1/25/03	2/1	February	Research, health pages
MARCH						
Women's History Month	Graphics Dept.	2/1	2/15/03 through 2/20/03	2/26	March	Home page, events

This editorial calendar is based on one that the author developed for the Las Vegas–Clark County Library District.

(continued)

EDITORIAL CALENDAR DATES and DEADLINES 2003						Last Revised 2/18/03
Event	*Contact*	*Submit*	*Review Period*	*Post*	*Event Date*	*Web Page*
MARCH						
Read across America	Graphics Dept.	2/5	2/20/02 through 3/10/03	3/14	March	Kid pages, events
Adult Reading Festival	Robin	3/1	3/15/03 through 3/20/03	3/24	4/1	Main; good reads
Freedom of Information Day	Janet	3/1	3/5/03 through 3/10/03	3/12	3/16	Home page
APRIL						
Earth Day	Ref. Comm.	4/1	4/10/03 through 4/15/03	4/18	4/20	Research pages
National Poetry Month	Teen Comm.	3/15	3/20/03 through 3/25/03	3/28	April	Teen pages
Easter Holiday	Graphics Dept.	4/1	4/2/03 through 4/5/03	4/7	4/20	Home page, events
National Library Month	Marketing, Ref. Comm.	3/25	3/28/03 through 3/31/03	4/2	4/6 through 4/12	Home page, events
MAY						
Asian Pacific American Heritage Month	Kim	4/3	3/10/03 through 3/17/03	4/21	May	Home page, events
Memorial Day	Graphics Dept.	5/7	5/10	5/12	5/26	Home page, events
JUNE						
Summer Reading Program	Deb	4/1	5/1/03 through 5/20/03	5/28	6/10 through 9/31	Home page, kid and teen pages
Children's Awareness Month	Ed	4/5	5/10/03 through 5/17/03	5/28	June	Kid and parent pages
JULY						
Fourth of July	Graphics Dept.	6/15	6/18/03 through 6/20/03	6/22	7/4	Feature
Harry Potter's Birthday	Youth Services Coordinator	7/1	7/5/03 through 7/12/03	7/20	7/31	Home page, kid and teen pages

EDITORIAL CALENDAR DATES and DEADLINES 2003						Last Revised 2/18/03
Event	*Contact*	*Submit*	*Review Period*	*Post*	*Event Date*	*Web Page*
AUGUST						
National Inventor's Month	Ref. Comm.	6/10	6/20/03 through 6/26/03	7/1	August	Research, special collections
Back to School	Youth Services	8/5	8/10/03 through 8/15/03	8/20	September	Home page, kid and teen pages
SEPTEMBER						
Hispanic Heritage Month	Adult Services Coordinator	8/1	8/16/03 through 8/25/03	8/30	September	Home page, events
Library Card Month	Circulation	8/5	8/12/03 through 8/17/03	8/20	September	Home page, library catalog
Banned Books Week	Reader's Advisory Comm.	8/20	9/1/03 through 9/8/03	9/10	9/20 through 9/27	Good reads
Labor Day	Graphics Dept.	8/12	8/14/03 through 8/16/03	8/18	9/1	Feature
OCTOBER						
National Breast Cancer Awareness Month	Health Librarian	9/10	9/19/03 through 9/22/03	9/25	October	Health pages
Teen Read Week	Teen Comm.	9/20	10/1/03 through 10/5/03	10/10	10/19/03 through 10/25/03	Teen pages
NOVEMBER						
Native American Heritage Month	Adult Services Coordinator	10/5	10/10/03 through 10/15/03	10/18	November	Home page, events
National Children's Book Week	Youth Services Coordinator	10/25	11/1/03 through 11/5/03	11/7	11/17/03 through 11/23/03	Kid and parent pages
Veterans' Day	Graphics Dept.	10/20	10/24/03 through 10/26/03	10/28	11/11	Feature
Thanksgiving	Graphics Dept.	11/6	11/8/03 through 11/10/03	11/13	11/27	Feature
Election Day	Ref. Comm.	10/1	10/18/03 through 10/22/03	10/25	11/4	Home page, research

(continued)

EDITORIAL CALENDAR DATES and DEADLINES 2003						Last Revised 2/18/03
Event	Contact	Submit	Review Period	Post	Event Date	Web Page
DECEMBER						
Holiday closing	Graphics Dept.	12/6	12/8/03 through 12/10/03	12/11	12/25	Feature

APPENDIX B

Library Web Manager's Resource Directory

ACCESSIBILITY

Bobby
http://bobby.watchfire.com

Creating Accessible Documents with
    Adobe Acrobat
http://www.adobe.com/products/
    acrobat/solutionsacc.html

Cynthia Says Portal
http://cynthia.contentquality.com

EASI (Easy Access to Software and
    Information)
http://www.rit.edu/~easi/index.htm

HTML Writers Guild's AWARE
(Accessible Web Authoring Resources
    and Education Center)
http://aware.hwg.org

Universal Access to Libraries
http://www.washington.edu/doit/UA/

W3C's Web Content Accessibility
    Guidelines 1.0
http://www.w3.org/TR/WAI-
    WEBCONTENT/

Data Enrichment Companies

Content Café
http://www.informata.com
704-329-2940

Syndetics Solutions
http://www.syndetics.com
877-737-9722

Free Resources from Vendors

EBSCO Publishing
http://www.epnet.com/freeres.asp

The Gale Group
http://www.galegroup.com/free_
    resources

E-JOURNAL LIST SERVICES AND LINK RESOLVERS

A-to-Z
EBSCO
http://atoz.ebsco.com
800-653-2726

A-to-Z Title List, Article Linker,
    and more
Serials Solutions
http://www.serialssolutions.com
866-737-4257

TDNet
http://www.tdnet.com/
888-705-3582

Link Resolvers within ILS Vendors

Millennium Access Plus: WebBridge
Innovative Interfaces, Inc.
http://www.iii.com/mill/digital.shtml
510-655-6200

SFX
Ex Libris
http://www.aleph.co.il/sfx/
877-527-1689

SIRSI Resolvers
SIRSI
http://www.sirsi.com/Sirsiproducts/
openurl.html
800-917-4774

ELECTRONIC BOOKS

Electronic Books in Libraries
http://www.lib.rochester.edu/main/
ebooks/index.htm

netLibrary
OCLC
http://www.netlibrary.com
800-848-5878

Overdrive.com
http://www.overdrive.com
216-573-6886

ILS PORTAL PRODUCTS

AGent Portal Module
Auto-Graphics
http://www4.auto-graphics.com/
product_agent.html
800-776-6939

Chameleon iPortal
VTLS, Inc.
http://www.vtls.com/Products/gateway/
800-468-8857

ENCompass Solutions
Endeavor
http://encompass.endinfosys.com/
whatis/whatisENC2.htm
800-762-6300

MetaLib
ExLibris (USA)
http://www.exlibris-
usa.com/MetaLib/index.html
877-527-1689

Millennium Access Plus
Innovative Interfaces
http://www.iii.com/mill/digital.shtml#
map

Polaris PowerPAC Portal
GIS Information Systems
http://www.gisinfosystems.com

YouSeeMore
The Library Corporation
http://www.tlcdelivers.com/tlccarl/
products/pacs/youseemore.asp

LINK CHECKERS

Doctor HTML
http://www.doctor-html.com/RxHTML

W3C's HTML Validator
http://validator.w3.org

Web Design Group's HTML Validator
http://www.htmlhelp.com/tools/
validator

ONLINE NEWSLETTERS

Association for Interactive Marketing
(AIM)
http://www.interactivemarketing.org

ClickZ
http://www.clickz.com

College Libraries' Newsletters—
A Webliography
http://www.ala.org/Content/Navigation
Menu/ACRL/About_ACRL/Sections/
College_Libraries/Publications18/
College_Libraries_Newsletters.htm

Netpreneur's AdMarketing
http://www.netpreneur.org

Opt-In News
http://www.optinnews.com

Wordbiz Report
http://www.wordbiz.com

RESOURCE INTEGRATION SERVICES

MuseSearch
MuseGlobal
http://www.museglobal.com/Products/
MuseSearch/index.html
801-208-1880

Resource Gateway
WebClarity
Sea Change Corporation
http://www.web-clarity.com
800-661-7274

Webfeat Knowledge Prism
Webfeat, Inc.
http://www.webfeat.org
888-757-9119

ZPORTAL
Fretwell-Downing
http://www.fdusa.com/products/
zportal.html
888-649-6542

SITE INDEXING SOFTWARE

ht://Dig
http://www.htdig.org
Web indexing and search software.
Free.

HTML Indexer
http://www.html-indexer.com
Creates a back-of-the-book index
from a collection of HTML files.

SWISH-E
http://www.swish-e.org
Indexes web pages and text files. Free.

USABILITY

Usability.gov
http://www.usability.gov

Usable Web
http://www.usableweb.com

useit.com: Jakob Nielsen's Website
http://www.useit.com

VIRTUAL REFERENCE

24/7 Reference
http://www.247ref.org
310-391-7444

QuestionPoint
OCLC
http://www.questionpoint.org
800-848-5878

Virtual Reference
LSSI
http://www.vrtoolkit.net
For more virtual reference links,
see LiveRef(sm), a Registry of Real-
Time Digital Reference Services
http://www.public.iastate.edu/
~CYBERSTACKS/LiveRef.htm

WEB DESIGN

Getty Images
http://www.gettyimages.com
877-438-8966

HTML Writers Guild
http://www.hwg.org

W3C World Wide Web Consortium
http://www.w3.org

Web Design Library—Builder.com
http://builder.cnet.com/webbuilding/
0-3884.html?tag=dir

Webdeveloper.com: All About Site
Management, Marketing, and
Analysis Tools
http://www.webdeveloper.com/
management

WEB MANAGEMENT

Issues in Creating and Managing
Library Websites
http://www.dpi.state.wi.us/dpi/dlcl/pld/
webguide.html

Library Web Manager's Reference
Center
http://sunsite.berkeley.edu/Web4Lib/
RefCenter

Web4Lib Electronic Discussion
http://sunsite.berkeley.edu/Web4Lib

WEB SITES

Alert Services

Best Free Reference Web Sites, RUSA
Machine-Assisted Reference
Section (MARS)
http://www.ala.org/Content/Navigation
Menu/RUSA/Our_Association2/
RUSA_Sections/MARS/Publications
13/MARSBestRef2003.htm

Best Information on the Net, St.
Ambrose University, O'Keefe Library
http://library.sau.edu/bestinfo/
Default.htm

The Internet Scout Project
http://scout.wisc.edu/

Librarian's Index to the Internet
http://www.lii.org

Neat New Stuff on the Net by
Marylaine Block
http://marylaine.com/neatnew.html

MARC Records

Dartclix
Brodart (500 Arch St., Williamsport,
PA 17701; 800-233-8467)
http://www.brodart.com

Provides collections of cataloged
web sites geared toward public and
school libraries. Includes grade levels within the 521 field.

Documents without Shelves
Marcive, Inc. (P.O. Box 47508,
San Antonio, TX 78265-7508;
800-531-7678)
http://www.marcive.com

Offers a subscription service of
hundreds of MARC records of full-
text online government documents.

Web Feet
Rock Hill Press (14 Rock Hill Rd.,
Bala Cynwyd, PA 19004;
888-762-5445)
http://www.webfeetguides.com

Offers a variety of collections of
MARC records for academic,
school, and public libraries, including a special collection of health
web sites.

WEB STATISTICS

NetTracker
Sane Solutions
http://www.sane.com/products/
   NetTracker/
800-407-3570

Web Trends
NetIQ
http://www.netiq.com/webtrends/
   default.asp
888-323-6768

WEB STYLE GUIDES

NYPL Online Style Guide
http://www.nypl.org/styleguide/

Web Style Guide, 2d ed.
http://www.webstyleguide.com/

Bibliography

American Library Association (ALA). 2003. *Overview: The children's online privacy protection act.* Available at http://www.ala.org/Template.cfm?Section= Childrens_Online_Privacy_Protection_Act_(COPPA)&Template=/Content Management/ContentDisplay.cfm&ContentID=11022.

American Library Association (ALA). Reference and Adult Services Division. Library Services to the Spanish Speaking Committee. 1988. *Guidelines for library services to Hispanics.* Available at http://www.ala.org/Content/ NavigationMenu/RUSA/Professional_Tools4/Reference_Guidelines/ Guidelines_for_Library_Services_to_Hispanics.htm.

American Library Association (ALA). Reference and User Services Association. 1999. *Library services to older adults guidelines.* Available at http:// www.ala.org/Content/NavigationMenu/RUSA/Professional_Tools4/ Reference_Guidelines/Library_Services_to_Older_Adults_Guidelines.htm.

American Library Association (ALA). Reference and User Services Association. 2000. *Guidelines for information services.* Available at http://www.ala.org/ Content/NavigationMenu/RUSA/Professional_Tools4/Reference_Guidelines/ Guidelines_for_Information_Services.htm.

American Library Association (ALA). Reference and User Services Association. 2001. *Guidelines for the preparation of a bibliography.* Available at http://www. ala.org/Content/NavigationMenu/RUSA/Professional_Tools4/Reference_ Guidelines/Guidelines_for_the_Preparation_of_a_Bibliography.htm.

Association of College and Research Libraries (ACRL). Instruction Section Teaching Methods Committee. 2003. *Tips for developing effective web-based library instruction.* Available at http://www.ala.org/Content/ ContentGroups/ACRL1/IS/ISCommittees/Web_pages/Teaching_ Methods/Tips.htm.

Association of Research Libraries. 2001. *Staffing the library web site.* SPEC Kit 266. Available at http://www.arl.org/spec/266sum.html.

Bayan, Ruby. 2001. Your global web site. *Link-Up* (September/October): 29.

Bickner, Carrie. 2002. Why web standards matter. *Library Journal netConnect* (summer): 26–28.

Boiko, Bob. 2001. *Content management bible.* New York: Wiley.

Boss, Richard W. 2002. How to plan and implement a library portal. *Library Technology Reports* (November/December): 1–53.

Brandt, D. Scott. 2001. Capitalizing on customer service redundancies. *Computers in Libraries* (September): 61–63.

Braun, Linda W. 2001. In virtual pursuit. *Library Journal netConnect* (fall): 32–34.

Braun, Linda W. 2002. *Teens.library: Developing Internet services for young adults.* Chicago: ALA.

Breeding, Marshall. 2001. Offering remote access to restricted resources. *Information Today* 18, no. 5. EBSCO, Professional Development Collection.

Browne, Glenda Michelle. 2001. Indexing web sites: A practical guide. *Internet Reference Services Quarterly* 5, no. 3: 27–41.

Caplan, Patricia L. 2001. A lesson in linking. *Library Journal netConnect* (fall): 16–18.

Center for Democracy and Technology. 2001. *How to read a privacy policy.* Available at http://www.consumerprivacyguide.org/howto/readpp.shtml.

Cherry, Joan M. 1998. Bibliographic displays in OPACs and web catalogs: How well do they comply with display guidelines? *Information Technology and Libraries* 17, no. 3 (September): 124–37.

Conrad, Debby, and Laurie Lessner. 2002. S.A.I.L.S. library network: Charting a course into the twenty-first century. *Computers in Libraries* (October): 23–25.

COUNTER. 2002. *COUNTER code of practice.* Available at http://www.projectcounter.org/code_practice.html.

Crawford, Walt. 1992. *The online catalog book: Essays and examples.* New York: Hall.

Crawford, Walt. 1999. Webcats and checklists: Some cautionary notes. *Information Technology and Libraries* 18, no. 2 (June): 100–103.

Creider, Laurence S. 2003. What are academic libraries doing with Spanish language subject headings? *Journal of Academic Librarianship* 29, no. 2 (March): 88–94.

Curtis, Donnelyn. 2002. *Attracting, educating, and serving remote users through the Web.* New York: Neal-Schuman.

Dictionary of computing. 1996. s.v. "Knowledge base." Oxford Reference Online.

Dodge, Bernie. 1998. *The webquest page.* Available at http://webquest.sdsu.edu/overview.htm.

Dowling, Thomas. 2003. Web manager's handbook. *Library Technology Reports* 39, no. 1. (January/February).

Downing, Arthur, and Leo Robert Klein. 2001. A multilingual virtual tour for international students: The web-based library at Baruch College opens doors. *College and Research Libraries News* 62, no. 5 (May): 500–502.

Durrance, Joan C., and Karen E. Pettigrew. 2002. *Online community information: Creating a nexus at your library.* Chicago: ALA.

EBSCO Publishing. n.d. *LinkSource: Definition of terms and frequently asked questions.* Available at http://www.ebscoweb.com/custsupport/ UserDocumentation/linksourcefaq.doc.

EBSCO Publishing. 2000. *Talking with readers: A workbook for readers' advisory.* Ipswich, Mass.: EBSCO.

Feldman, Sari, and Tracy Strobel. 2002. *Advancing your library's web-based services.* Syracuse, N.Y.: ERIC Clearinghouse on Information and Technology. EBSCO, ERIC, ED 456379.

Friedlander, Amy. 2002. *Dimensions and use of the scholarly information environment.* Washington, D.C.: Digital Library Federation and Council on Library and Information Resources. Available at http://www.clir.org/pubs/reports/ pub110/contents.html.

Friedlein, Ashley. 2000. *Web project management: Delivering successful commercial web sites.* Orlando, Fla.: Morgan Kaufmann.

Garner, Jane, Lynne Horwood, and Shirley Sullivan. 2001. *Examining one model of ebooks for an academic library setting.* Available at http://www.vala.org.au/ vala2002/2002pdf/35GaHoSu.pdf.

Green, Elisabeth. 1998. Web-based catalogs: Is their design language anything to talk about? *Online* (July/August). Available at http://www.findarticles.com.

Grogg, Jill E., and Christine L. Ferguson. 2003. Linking services unleashed. *Searcher* 11, no. 2 (February): 26–31.

Guenther, Kim. 2003. Protecting your web site, protecting your users. *Online* (May/June): 63–66.

Hackos, Joann T. 2002. *Content management for dynamic web delivery.* New York: Wiley.

Hammerich, Irene, and Claire Harrison. 2001. *Developing online content: The principles of writing and editing for the Web.* New York: Wiley.

Himmel, Ethel, and William James Wilson. 1998. *Planning for results.* Chicago: ALA.

Horrigan, John B., and Lee Rainie. 2002. *Counting on the Internet.* Washington, D.C.: Pew Internet and American Life Project. Available at http://www. pewinternet.org/reports/pdfs/PIP_Expectations.pdf.

IBM Corporation. *What is user-centered design?* Available at http://www-3.ibm. com/ibm/easy/eou_ext.nsf/Publish/2.

International Federation of Library Associations and Institutions (IFLA). 2002. *Digital reference standards project.* Available at http://www.ifla.org/VII/s36/ pubs/drsp.htm.

Kaye, H. S. 2000. Computer and Internet use among people with disabilities. *Disability Statistics Report* (13). Washington D.C.: U.S. Department of Education, National Institute on Disability and Rehabilitation Research. Available at http://www.dsc.ucsf.edu.

Kelly, James M. 2000. Promoting fiction: Readers' advisory and the use of the public library web sites. Master's thesis, University of North Carolina, Chapel Hill.

Kennedy, Shirley Duglin. 2000. Linking policies for public web sites. *Information Today* 17, no. 10 (November): 42–43.

Kim, Heesop, Hyunsoo Chung, Gichai Hong, Byungju Moon, and Chee-Hang Park. 1999. Correlations between users' characteristics and preferred features of web-based OPAC evaluation. *ETRI Journal* 21, no. 4 (December): 83–93.

Kimen, Shel. 1999. *Ten questions about information architecture.* Available at http://builder.cnet.com/webbuilding/0-3881-8-5113200-9.html.

Kirkpatrick, Cheryl H. 2003. Getting two for the price of one: Accessibility and usability. *Computers in Libraries* 23, no. 1 (January): 27–29.

Klein, Leo Robert. 2002. On the same page. *Library Journal netConnect* (winter): 12–14. Available at http://libraryjournal.reviewsnews.com/index.asp?layout= article&articleid=CA190392.

Klein, Leo Robert. 2003. Mixing up web site management. *Library Journal netConnect* 128, no. 7 (spring): 28–30.

Kupersmith, John. 2002. *Terms found on usability-tested library home pages.* Available at http://www.jkup.net/terms-on-tested-pages.html.

Kupersmith, John. 2003. *Library terms that users understand.* Available at http:// www.jkup.net/terms.html.

Latham, Joyce M. 2002. To link, or not to link. *Library Journal* 127, no. 7 (April 15): 20–22.

Lenhart, Amanda, Lee Rainie, and Oliver Lewis. 2001. *Teenage life online: The rise of the instant-message generation and the Internet's impact on friendships and family relationships.* Washington, D.C.: Pew Internet and American Life Project. Available at http://www.pewinternet.org/reports/pdfs/PIP_Teens_ Report.pdf.

Library Information and Technology Association (LITA). 2002. *The top trends.* Available at http://www.lita.org/committe/toptech/annual02.htm.

Lynch, Patrick J., and Sarah Horton. 2002. *Web style guide: Basic design principles for creating web sites.* 2d ed. New Haven: Yale University.

Mach, Michelle, and Jennifer S. Kutzik. 2001. The web is everyone's business: A distributed system for managing the library web site. *Colorado Libraries* 27 (fall): 29–32.

McConnell, Mike, and Iain A. Middleton. 2002. Centralisation or departmental freedom? Presented at the *Institutional Web Management Workshop*. Available at http://www.ukoln.ac.uk/web-focus/events/workshops/ webmaster-2002/talks/mcconnell/.

McGovern, Gerry, Rob Norton, and Catherine O'Dowd. 2001. *The web content style guide: An essential reference for online writers, editors and managers.* Upper Saddle River, N.J.: Prentice-Hall.

Meola, Marc, and Sam Stormont. 2002. *Starting and operating live virtual reference services: A how-to-do-it manual for librarians.* New York: Neal-Schuman.

MIT Libraries Web Advisory Group. *Card-sorting exercise: Results, pt. 1.* Available at http://Macfadden.mit.edu:9500/webgroup/cards/results.html.

Morrissett, Linda A. 1994. Leisure reading in academic libraries: A survey. *North Carolina Libraries* 52 (fall/winter): 122–25.

Nakano, Russell. 2001. *Web content management: A collaborative approach.* Boston: Addison-Wesley.

National Cancer Institute. n.d. *Usability.gov: Methods for designing usable web sites.* Available at http://usability.gov/methods/type_of_test.html.

National Institute of Standards and Technology (NIST). Convergent Information Systems Division. 2003. *Products.* Available at http://www.itl.nist.gov/div895/ products.html.

National School Boards Foundation. n.d. *Research and guidelines for children's use of the Internet.* Available at http://www.nsbf.org/safe-smart/ full-report.htm.

NetRatings. 2003. *Nielsen/NetRatings Top twenty-five parent companies.* Available at http://www.netratings.com/news.jsp?section=dat_to&country=us.

Nielsen, Jakob. 2000. *Designing web usability.* Indianapolis: New Riders.

Nielsen, Jakob. 2002. Site map usability. *Alertbox.* Available at http://www. useit.com/alertbox/20020106.html.

Nielsen, Jakob, and Marie Tahir. 2002. *Homepage usability: Fifty websites deconstructed.* Indianapolis: New Riders.

Nordmeyer, Ricki. 2001. Readers' advisory web sites. *Reference and User Services Quarterly* 41, no. 2 (winter): 139–43.

OCLC Online Computer Library Center. Office of Research. 2002. *OCLC web characterization.* Available at http://wcp.oclc.org.

Ortiz-Repiso, Virginia, and Purificacion Moscoso. 1999. Web-based OPACs: Between tradition and innovation. *Information Technology and Libraries* 18, no. 2: 68–77. Also available from OCLC FirstSearch, WilsonSelect Plus.

Oxford English dictionary. 2d ed. 1989. Edited by J. A. Simpson and E. S. C. Weiner. Additions 1993–97. Edited by John Simpson, Edmund Weiner, and Michael Proffitt. 3d ed. (in progress). March 2000– . Edited by John Simpson. OED Online. Oxford: Oxford University Press.

Pace, Andrew K. 2003. The usability toolbox. *Computers in Libraries* 23, no. 1 (January): 52.

Parkhurst, Carol A. 2002. Supporting the remote user of licensed resources. In *Attracting, educating, and serving remote users through the Web.* New York: Neal-Schuman.

Pew Internet and American Life Project. 2001. *The Internet and education.* Available at http://www.pewinternet.org/reports/pdfs/PIP_Schools_Report.pdf.

Pew Internet and American Life Project. 2001. *Teenage life online: The rise of the instant-message generation and the Internet's impact on friendships and family relationships.* Available at http://www.pewinternet.org/reports/pdfs/PIP_Teens_Report.pdf.

Pew Internet and American Life Project. 2002a. *The digital disconnect: The widening gap between Internet-savvy students and their schools.* Available at http://www.pewinternet.org/reports/toc.asp?Report=67.

Pew Internet and American Life Project. 2002b. *Search engines: A Pew Internet project data memo.* Available at http://www.pewinternet.org/reports/pdfs/PIP_Search_Engine_Data.pdf.

Porter, G. Margaret, and Laura Bayard. 1999. Including web sites in the online catalog: Implications for cataloging, collection development, and access. *The Journal of Academic Librarianship* 25, no. 5 (September): 390–94.

Purdy, Rebecca. 2002. Web sites for young adults and their librarians. *VOYA* 25, no. 4 (October): 262–63.

Reiss, Eric L. 2000. *Practical information architecture: A hands-on approach to structuring successful websites.* Boston: Addison-Wesley.

Rosenfeld, Louis, and Peter Morville. 2002. *Information architecture for the World Wide Web.* 2d ed. Sebastopol, Calif.: O'Reilly.

SeniorNet. 2002. *SeniorNet survey on Internet use.* Available at http://www.seniornet.org/php/default.php?PageID=6880&Version=0&Font=0.

Smith, Susan Sharpless. 2001. *Web-based instruction: A guide for libraries.* Chicago: ALA.

Stewart, Ron. 2003. *Accessibility of online databases: A usability study of research databases.* Available at http://tap.oregonstate.edu/research/ahg.htm.

Tenopir, Carol. 2003. *Use and users of electronic library resources: An overview and analysis of recent research studies.* Washington, D.C.: Council on Library and Information Resources. Available at http://www.clir.org.

Tillman, Hope. *Evaluating quality on the net.* 2003. Available at http://www. hopetillman.com/findqual.html.

Traw, Jeri L., comp. 2000. *Library web site policies.* CLIP note no. 29. Chicago: ALA.

University of Washington. 2001. *Making library resources accessible to people with disabilities.* Available at http://www.washington.edu/doit/Brochures/ Technology/libsrv.html.

University of Wisconsin Law Library. (2002). *About this site.* Available at http://library.law.wisc.edu/aboutsite.htm.

U.S. Bureau of the Census. 2000a. *Disability status by sex: 2000.* Data set: Census 2000 Summary File 3 (SF 3) Sample Data. Available at http://www.census.gov.

U.S. Bureau of the Census. 2000b. *Language spoken at home for the population five years and over, 2000. Supplementary Survey Summary Tables P034.* Available at http://www.census.gov.

U.S. Bureau of the Census. 2001. *Home computers and Internet use in the United States: Current population reports P23-20, 2000.* Available at http://www. census.gov/population/www/socdemo/computer.html.

U.S. General Services Administration Center for IT Accommodation (CITA) Office of Governmentwide Policy. 2002. Web-based intranet and Internet information and applications. Available at http://www.section508.gov/index. cfm?FuseAction=Content&ID=12#Web.

U.S. National Library of Medicine. 2001. *Making your web site senior friendly.* Available at http://www.nlm.nih.gov/pubs/checklist.pdf.

U.S. National Telecommunications and Information Administration. 2002. *A nation online: How Americans are expanding their use of the Internet.* Available at http://www.ntia.doc.gov/ntiahome/dn/Nation_Online.pdf.

U.S. 1998 amendment to section 508 of the Rehabilitation Act. Rehabilitation Act (29 U.S.C. 794d), Section 508, as amended by the Workforce Investment Act of 1998 (P.L. 105-220), August 7, 1998. Available at http://www. section508.gov/index.cfm?FuseAction=Content&ID=14.

Usborne, Nick. 2001. *Net words: Creating high-impact online copy.* New York: McGraw-Hill.

Valenza, Joyce Kasman. 2000. Surfing blind. *Library Journal netConnect* 125, no. 14 (fall): 34–36.

Vaughan, Jason. 2001. Three iterations of an academic library web site. *Information Technology and Libraries* 20, no. 2 (June): 81–92.

Vesper, Virginia. n.d. *The readers' advisor in academic libraries.* Available at http://www.mtsu.edu/~vvesper/advise.html.

World Wide Web Consortium (W3C). 1999. *Web content accessibility guidelines 1.0.* Available at http://www.w3.org/TR/1999/WAI-WEBCONTENT-19990505.

Zauha, Janelle M. 1993. Personal reading in academic browsing rooms. *Collection Building* 12, nos. 3–4: 57–62.

Zeng, Marcia Lei. 2001. Making indexes for web sites: A taste of the challenge. *Key Words* 9, no. 2 (March/April): 43–45.

Index